ENOUGH
FAITH

DR. KEN HUTCHERSON

Multnomah® Publishers *Sisters, Oregon*

ENOUGH FAITH
published by Multnomah Publishers, Inc.

© 2006 by Ken Hutcherson
International Standard Book Number: 1-59052-600-7

Cover design by The DesignWorks Group, Inc.
Cover photo by Teresa Roorback

Unless otherwise indicated, Scripture quotations are from:
The Holy Bible, New King James Version
© 1984 by Thomas Nelson, Inc.
Other Scripture quotations are from:
The Holy Bible, New International Version (NIV)
© 1973, 1984 by International Bible Society,
used by permission of Zondervan Publishing House
The Amplified Bible (AMP)
© 1965, 1987 by Zondervan Publishing House.
Holy Bible, New Living Translation (NLT)
© 1996. Used by permission of Tyndale House Publishers, Inc.
All rights reserved.

Multnomah is a trademark of Multnomah Publishers, Inc.,
and is registered in the U.S. Patent and Trademark Office.
The colophon is a trademark of Multnomah Publishers, Inc.

For information:
MULTNOMAH PUBLISHERS, INC.
601 N. LARCH ST.
SISTERS, OREGON 97759

Library of Congress Cataloging-in-Publication Data

Hutcherson, Ken.
  Enough faith / Ken Hutcherson.
    p. cm.
  ISBN 1-59052-600-7
  1. Faith. 2. Christian life. I. Title.
  BV4637.H86 2006
  234'.23--dc22

                                      2006000690

06 07 08 09 10 11—10 9 8 7 6 5 4 3 2 1 0

Dedication

In memory of one of my greatest disciples David Brown, one of the original Seattle Seahawks, who went to be with our Lord in January, 2006. He was a man that lived fully the faith that he already had and influenced more men to walk with Christ as he did. I love you, Bro, and will see you on my arrival.

CONTENTS

Prologue

JUST TO GET YOU STARTED...

I f you've got enough faith to get you *Here*, you've got enough faith to get you *There*.

Do you believe that?

So where is *Here*?

Here is where you are right now, if by faith you have received God's free gift of salvation by accepting the Lord Jesus Christ as your Savior. If you're really *Here*, then you have been snatched from the kingdom of darkness and placed securely forever in the kingdom of light. *Here* means you have been released from the chains of Satan and his army of evil angels, you've been given eternal life, and you have been adopted as a beloved son or daughter into God's intimate family circle.

That's *Here*.

And *Here* is amazing.

But how did you get *Here*?

You got *Here* by placing your faith in Christ to save you, make you alive, and restore you. Now *Here* you are, in the same forever-family with Abraham, Isaac, Jacob, Moses, Esther, Jeremiah, John the Baptizer, and all the saints through all the ages.

Tell me…how much faith did it take to get you *Here*? Who can say? All you know is that it was enough. You had enough faith to get *Here*, and *Here* you are, a son or daughter of the living God.

Now…where is *There*?

There is what you're moving into as you live out your life day by day. *There* is all the troubles and trials and opportunities and challenges and choices God places before you on any given Sunday through Saturday. *There* can be pretty challenging sometimes, amen? *There* can be hard to bear. Your heart can be broken *There*. You can encounter mountains on your way to *There*. You can run into brick walls and dead ends and disappointments. You can find yourself in situations that seem way beyond your strength, wisdom, or experience. *There* can be a scary place.

Sometimes people say the reason you can't succeed *There* is because you need "more faith." You encounter an obstacle, you find yourself facing a challenge, and you turn back, thinking you "don't have enough faith." And then you grieve and mourn because it's so hard to muster up more faith. So you tell yourself God can't really use you after all—unless, somehow, somewhere you could find more faith.

But that's a lie.

We've been taught "more faith, more faith, more faith" so often. You can look through the whole Bible and not find this concept of "needing more faith." The Bible says, "You've either got it, or you don't!"

God says to us, "Do you want to do great things for Me? You don't need more faith. If you could get *Here* by trusting Me for salvation, you can certainly get *There*." Don't lose heart, regardless of what happens. If you can ask a holy God to come into your life, forgive you, and change your eternal destination on faith alone, apart from any effort or works of your own, then that is the greatest faith in all the world. Everything else is downhill!

The fact is, you have all the faith you will ever need. What greater miracle could there be than receiving Jesus and passing from eternal death and damnation to eternal life? What situation or circumstance could you encounter that would require more faith than that?

What you need to do is to make sure you're walking in the faith you already have.

Remember when Peter, James, and John came down off the mountain where they had caught a glimpse of Jesus in His glory? The nine remaining disciples had run into a quandary. The father of a demon- possessed boy had brought his son to the nine followers of Jesus, and they couldn't heal him.

Jesus became angry. Turning to the nine, He said, "O faithless and perverse generation, how long shall I be with you? How long shall I bear with you? Bring him here to Me" (Matthew 17:17).

Later, when the disciples came to Jesus and asked why they couldn't cast out the demon, Jesus told them, "Because of your unbelief" (v. 20).

What is "unbelief" to a believer? It is when you become so weak and passive in the faith you already have that you neglect or refuse to take the next step with it. You go backwards. You lose ground. Faith, like a muscle that never gets moved or exercised, shrinks and shrivels. And that's what had happened to the disciples. They had already experienced the power of Jesus surging through them way back in Matthew 10:1.

> And when He had called His twelve disciples to Him, He gave
> them power over unclean spirits, to cast them out, and to heal
> all kinds of sickness and all kinds of disease.

They had faith then. They had already experienced healing the sick and sending demons running for cover. But by Matthew 17, they had let that faith grow weak. They didn't need "more faith" to cast out the demon, they needed to return to what they'd left behind.

It's the same for us. If we have faith to get us *Here*, then it's all the faith we need to get us *There*, whatever challenges you may be facing right now, wherever *There* may be for you.

God's challenge to us? Don't become weak! Don't retreat! Don't falter! Don't turn back! If you had faith once, don't let it drain away. Keep it strong. Go forward. Take the next step. Do the next thing.

When you married that man, when you married that woman, did you have enough faith to say, "I do"? Did you have enough faith to believe God would give you strength to be a good husband or a good wife through all the years "until death do us part"? If you had enough faith to do that, then you have enough faith to remain faithful, and to stand by your spouse no matter what situations, trials, or challenges you may face in your marriage.

You don't lose faith; you lose the will to walk in your faith.

Jesus told His disciples, "Assuredly, I say to you, if you have faith as a mustard seed, you will say to this mountain, 'Move from here to there,' and it will move; and nothing will be impossible for you" (Matthew 17:20).

A mustard seed of faith will move a mountain. What are we talking about here? Mount Rainier? Mount Kilimanjaro? Probably not. You really don't see any mountain-moving going on in Scripture. The mountains in the Bible all stayed put. Jesus was giving His men a picture. He was talking about anything that seems huge and intimidating and unmovable in our lives. Any problem, any situation, any difficulty, any shortfall, any obstacle, any worry.

Don't let those mountains get in your way, Jesus was saying. And why should you? Responding to the mustard-seed faith you already have, God moved you out from under a mountain of despair and condemnation, and lifted you to the heights of joy, salvation, healing, cleansing, power, and a life that will outlast the stars and planets.

You don't need more faith, my friend.

You need to hold on to the faith you have.

You need to take that faith, whatever its size, and plant it in the strength and faithfulness of almighty God.

If He was strong enough to bring you *Here*, He's got strength to spare to get you *There*!

Introduction

"LITTLE" FAITH GOES A LONG WAY

She wheeled her way up to me after one of our early Sunday services crying her eyes out. When she told me her story, it broke my heart.

It also made me angry.

It wasn't this wheelchair-bound young woman's disability that bothered me, and it wasn't that she hadn't been healed. I know my God well enough to understand that He sometimes allows people He loves to go through tough times when it suits His purposes, which are always for our best. What really troubled me was some of the things some well-meaning but very misguided Christians had been telling her about her disability. This dear young woman—a woman who loved God and believed in Him as the God who keeps all His promises—had fallen victim to some popular but very unsound teaching.

For years and years she'd been told that the reason she wasn't able to get up out of her wheelchair and walk was because she "didn't have enough faith to be healed." And because she believed what she had been told, she'd been carrying a load of guilt and sorrow over her "little faith."

Right off the top, let me say that I certainly do believe in a wonder-working God of miracles who heals people when He desires. The God who created the intricacies of the human body can certainly heal it—in an instant—whenever He chooses to. But I also believe that He doesn't *always* choose to. He didn't in the Old Testament. He didn't in the New Testament. And He doesn't now. The truth is, there are times when God allows His sons and daughters to remain in terrible physical straits simply because—for reasons only He understands—He chooses not to raise them up yet. And until He moves to change our situations, it doesn't matter how much faith we have, because we'll stay where we are for as long as He wants us there (2 Corinthians 12:7–10.)

I'm not the first pastor to be angered and grieved over bad teaching. If you read the book of Galatians, you find Paul almost beside himself, he was so upset over the false teachers and twisted doctrines that had slipped into the church he had founded with his own blood, sweat, and tears. These teachers were loading up weights on the backs of the brothers and sisters that they were never, never meant to bear.

So Paul got really angry.

And so do I.

It deeply disturbs me when I meet so many Christians walking around today under a load of guilt because of unbalanced, unbiblical teaching. They can't look another believer in the eyes because they've been taught that the only reason they haven't been healed—physically, emotionally, or relationally—is because they didn't beg, borrow, or steal "enough faith" to make it happen.

And it goes beyond healing.

They're also told they need "more faith" to be a good spouse, a wise parent, an effective employee, and a faithful witness for Christ. When it doesn't happen...well, they feel defeated and deficient. Second-class Christians.

What upsets me most about this kind of teaching is that it directly contradicts something Jesus told His twelve disciples at the very moment they were facing a "crisis of faith" of their own: "Assuredly, I say to you, if you have faith as a mustard seed, you will say to this mountain, 'Move from here to there,' and it will move; and nothing will be impossible for you" (Matthew 17:20).

Jesus calls all of us to live lives of faith. He calls us to simply believe in a God who keeps all His promises and who responds to us, *when we put the little faith we have in Him.* You see, it doesn't take a large amount of faith on our part for God to do great things on our behalf. No, it takes a little faith—faith the size of a tiny seed—in a big God who is able to do far beyond what we even dare ask for.

Too many believers make the mistake of building their "devotional lives"—those times they set aside for reading the Word, meditating, and praying—around trying to acquire more faith.

And that, I believe, is exactly backwards.

When we take the attitude that we've got to have more faith in order to get God to do what we need or want Him to do, then we're putting the focus on *ourselves,* not Him. We become worried and preoccupied about what we can do, instead of filling our hearts up with the God who can move mountains on our behalf.

Do you want this whole book in a nutshell? Here it

is: *It's not the amount of faith we have that matters. What matters is what we do with the faith God has given us.* What matters is putting the faith we have—be it great or small—in a big God, knowing He will keep all His promises and do what He has said He will do. When we focus ourselves that way, we can look at the mountains in our path and know that whether or not God moves them, our little faith in Jesus Christ will give us all we need to get through the situation. *Any* situation.

I hope that as you read through this book you will see that God never called anyone to have a "big" faith, just a faith that is completely, radically placed in Him and in His Word. Even more than that, I hope you will understand that putting that little faith in Him will make a *huge* difference—in your life and in the lives of those God brings into your world.

How much faith do we really need?

What if you found out you have all you need already?

Well, read on, and let's check it out!

1

MUSTARD-SEED FAITH

Have you ever been faced with a situation so serious and so difficult that you didn't know if you could even handle it? Has God ever asked you to do something you knew very well was beyond your ability to deal with on your own? Have you ever looked at something God has brought to your attention and wondered how you—just one man or woman—could possibly do anything to influence or change it?

If you're wrestling with questions like these, I think God might have you right where He wants you. And where is that? He's got you in a place where nothing but your faith in Him and His power will do.

The time to be concerned in your Christian life is not when you are faced with impossible obstacles. The time to be concerned is when you find yourself thinking, *I don't need to pray. I can handle this. That* is the time to worry!

Jesus spent most of His earthly ministry preparing His disciples to face the impossible. His first call had been to follow Him, but that was just the beginning. After traveling with Him for three years—watching, listening, and learning—they would go on to do amazing things for the kingdom of God. It wasn't going to be easy, but it would be more than possible for them— once they had learned to live, breathe, speak, and walk in this thing called faith.

STORY TIME

There came a point in Jesus' time with the disciples that His teaching methods changed. Instead of talking to them directly and to the point, He began using parables to teach them. These stories—Jesus' way of giving the disciples eternal spiritual messages—were based on everyday things they could readily understand.

Why do you suppose He did that? Why did He make it more difficult for people to understand what He was really saying? The disciples themselves wanted an answer to that question, and Jesus explained it this way: "It has been given to you to know the mysteries of the kingdom of heaven, but to them it has not been given. For whoever has, to him more will be given, and he will have abundance; but whoever does not have, even what he has will be taken away from him" (Matthew 13:11–12).

In other words, Jesus was telling them, "Fellas, I have something of eternal value to say, but I'm only going say it to those who are committed to following Me and to continuing on in what I've started after I'm gone."

At the very time when the Lord was explaining His reasons for teaching in parables, a number of His followers were packing it in, giving up on Jesus. People were leaving Him; even His family was thinking He'd lost His mind. But in the midst of all that, Jesus began giving the disciples teaching that would encourage them to have enough faith to hold on and hold fast to Him, no matter what came their way.

That is the same encouragement He gives us today.

TINY SEED, GIGANTIC TREE

The thirteenth chapter of Matthew's Gospel includes not only Jesus' reasons for teaching in parables, but seven examples of these stories. In this chapter, I want to focus on two of them: the Parable of the Mustard Seed and the Parable of Yeast (or Leaven).

Here's the Parable of the Mustard Seed, which teaches an important lesson about what it means to have "enough faith":

> "The kingdom of heaven is like a mustard seed, which a man took and sowed in his field, which indeed is the least of all the seeds; but when it is grown it is greater than the herbs and becomes a tree, so that the birds of the air come and nest in its branches."
>
> MATTHEW 13:31-32

Whenever you read one of Jesus' parables, you can know that there's more to it than meets the eye. In this story, Jesus is saying that God can make something big out of something very small. In other words, God can take the small gifts you have—especially your faith—and do something great with them. And what is our responsibility in that equation?

We need to plant what we have. We need to put it to work.

If He's given us an itty-bitty mustard seed of faith, we need to plant it where God says to plant it, nurture it the way He says to nurture it, and then watch as it grows into something bigger and more powerful than we might have hoped or dreamed.

This is a truth we can abide in today, and a truth that has proven itself throughout history.

The most important movements in history—good and evil alike—didn't start with meetings. They didn't start with committees, sub-committees, study panels, or symposiums. Most of them started with one person's small idea—and a passionate belief in what that person was doing.

For example, the Third Reich—the very embodiment of human evil—started when one man had a vision, a warped and wicked vision. The Third Reich didn't start through meetings and committees, but with the twisted ideas of Adolph Hitler, who had a vision for world domination and the extermination of people he had come to believe represented a threat to German society.

Now there have been some great and very positive movements that have started because one individual—or maybe just a few—had a vision and went with it, even in the face of what seemed like overwhelming odds. One of my favorite examples of that is a man named William Wilberforce.

If you don't know about William Wilberforce, you need to, because he is an example of what can happen when a Christian plants a mustard seed of faith, then perseveres until the seed takes root. Because Wilberforce did just that, he is remembered to this day as a giant of the faith.

William Wilberforce was a young British man with great political aspirations. Elected to parliament in the late 1700s, he turned out to be instrumental in abolishing the slave trade in the British Empire. Wilberforce wasn't the only one in England who wanted to see the slave trade stopped, but he was part of a very small minority.

Wilberforce had become a Christian several years before his election to parliament, and had become convinced that trading precious humans for the purpose of slavery was both immoral and ungodly. One of the men Wilberforce had conversed with was John Newton, the former slave trader who had given his life to Christ and was now working with others to abolish the trafficking of human lives. (Newton, if you didn't know, was the writer of the beloved hymn "Amazing Grace.")

"So enormous, so dreadful, so irremediable did the [slave] Trade's wickedness appear that my own mind was completely made up for Abolition," Wilberforce wrote in his later years. "Let the consequences be what they would, I from this time determined that I would never rest until I had effected its abolition."

It was a noble idea. But it wasn't going to be easy.

At that time, English slave traders were capturing tens of thousands of Africans every year and shipping them off to be sold into bondage. Many, if not most, people believed that the British economy couldn't survive without the use of slaves. Wilberforce knew that making the trade illegal in the Empire would be extremely difficult and would require him to persevere through all sorts of opposition.

That's exactly what happened, too. Wilberforce submitted draft after draft of legislation to outlaw the trade of slaves in the British Empire, only to see them shot down in the parliament. Not only that, he was ruthlessly ridiculed, both by his fellow parliamentarians—many of whom refused to even talk to him—and by the British press.

But William Wilberforce believed too deeply in what he was trying to do to give up. Instead of throwing in the towel, he brought to his side others who shared his faith in God and views about the slave trade.

In time, what had started out as a mustard seed of opposition to the slave trade began growing into a powerful movement. Over the years, the makeup of the British parliament changed, as more and more men who shared Wilberforce's views on the slave trade were being elected.

Finally, in 1807, after nearly two decades of fighting what he knew was a good and righteous fight, Wilberforce's own mustard seed grew into a full-grown tree. He and his fellow anti-slave trade parliamentarians submitted a draft to abolish the trade in the Empire. But this time, he wasn't met with jeers and laughter from the other parliamentarians. Instead, member after member arose to voice his support and to praise Wilberforce for his perseverance. When the vote finally came, the motion to abolish the slave trade in the British Empire passed overwhelmingly. Now, it was only a matter of time before not just the slave trade but slavery itself would be a thing of the past in the British realm.

At the passing of Wilberforce's measure, the entire parliament arose to pay tribute to him. By this time he was so exhausted and sick he could only sit, with tears streaming down his face, and listen as his fellow parliamentarians applauded him and the others who had played a part in finally seeing the British slave trade abolished.

God had given William Wilberforce the seed of a vision. He caught a glimpse of the way things needed to be in his country, and because he had the faith to plant that seed, it grew into something that only twenty years before seemed impossible.

Now I've mentioned two important historic movements—one extremely negative and evil, and one extremely positive and good—because I wanted you to understand that world-shaking things can come out of the visions and faith of one individual. But I also want you to understand another principle of faith: The *kinds* of seeds you plant can make all the difference.

WHAT KIND OF SEEDS?

There is a principle woven throughout the pages of the Bible, one that the apostle Paul laid out directly and with simplicity: "Do not be deceived: God cannot be mocked. A man reaps what he sows. The one who sows to please his sinful nature, from that nature will reap destruction; the one who sows to please the Spirit, from the Spirit will reap eternal life" (Galatians 6:7–8, NIV).

We all know that it's a law of nature that you'll harvest the same kind of crop that you put into the ground. If you're planting a big field of corn, you're not going to be harvesting bushels of wheat from that same field. And if you plant tomatoes, you shouldn't expect to be picking green beans later on.

It's like that in the spiritual realm, too—and that's why we need to be very careful what kind of "faith seeds" we sow. Jesus promised us that this whole mustard-seed faith thing works in a powerful, positive way. But we need to be aware that it also works in the negative, too.

Jesus wanted His disciples to know that it only took a little faith on their parts to do great things for the kingdom of God. He told them, "Assuredly, I say to you, if you have faith as a mustard seed, you will say to this mountain, 'Move from here to there,' and it will move; and nothing will be impossible for you" (Matthew 17:20).

The very fact that you are sitting where you are reading those words—two thousand years later and probably half a world away from the time and place where Jesus spoke them—tells you that everything He said to His disciples about mustard-seed faith is true.

Eleven of Jesus' original twelve apostles eventually took hold of what Jesus was saying about planting small seeds of faith. As a result, the world was changed. The greatest movement in human history spread from the city of Jerusalem around the globe.

That's a principle all Christians need to understand and apply in their walk of faith today. But it's one I think too many of us apply in the negative. How many of us have looked at something we know God wants us to do—and has the power to make happen—and said, "I don't think it's going to work"?

It's not going to work between my spouse and me.

It's not going to do me any good to pray for my father's salvation. He's hard as a rock.

It's not going to help anyone for me to boldly proclaim Jesus Christ to people around me. People are cynical about Jesus.

It's not going to make any difference if I speak out about biblical morality and the sanctity of life in my city. I'm just one voice.

All of the statements above are planting negative

seeds of faith, and they are seeds that are sure to grow in the soil of our doubt and unbelief. You plant them, and you reap the harvest.

What kind of seeds are we planting today? Are we planting those tiny mustard seeds of faith in what God has promised us through His written Word, or are we planting seeds of negativity and unbelief? Are we planting seeds of obedience, even in the face of difficulties and opposition, or are we planting seeds of cynicism and disobedience?

It's a biblical truth that whatever we plant is going to grow and multiply—sometimes beyond our control. That's why we can't plant seeds of negativity, cynicism, and disobedience and not expect to deal with the consequences of that planting.

NEGATIVE SEEDS, DITTO THE CROPS

We Christians have reason to have all the hope in the world, but too many of us sit around and mope. We're like the old cartoon character Bad Luck Schleprock, who had bad things happen to him all the time because he believed they would.

If you want a real-life example, you shouldn't have to look beyond your own circle of friends. We've all known people who have a sickly attitude or who worry constantly about coming down with something. They hear about some exotic disease on TV or the radio, and immediately start feeling all the symptoms. Well, guess what usually happens to people like that? They actually do become sick! All that fretting and worrying about getting sick becomes a self-fulfilling prophecy. Their bodies may be perfectly healthy, but in their minds they are sickly and weak.

You know, I just love how science and medicine confirm what the Bible has already told us. One example of this—and it applies to the principle of mustard-seed faith—is how our attitudes can affect our health. People who live their lives with a positive attitude are usually healthier, both in mind and body, than those who walk around all stressed-out and worried about everything. On the other hand, those who allow their worries, fears, and stress to rule them are far more likely to suffer from all kinds of physical problems.

This is one of the reasons I don't like being around negative people (that and the fact that it just isn't much fun). These are the kind of people who can just suck all the optimism and good feelings out of a room the minute they walk in. They don't even have to open their mouths. You can sense their attitude and read the expression on their faces. They can't imagine anything good happening, and even if it did happen, they would be waiting for "the other shoe to drop." Sadly enough, these are the kinds of people who regularly fill our churches on Sunday mornings.

That reminds me of a joke about a little boy who walked with his father down the hallways of their church one Sunday morning, where the lad saw photographs of men lining the walls. "Daddy, who are all these people?" the boy asked. "Well, son, these are people who died in the service," answered the dad. The boy looked at his father and asked, "Which one? The first or the second?"

Now where do you think that little boy got the idea people were dying in the church services? Probably from the frowning, unhappy faces he saw in the pews each week. Why are they frowning? Because they can't leave their problems in God's hands and just live as if they really believed that His words are true, and that He keeps each and every promise He has ever made them. These are people who have sown seeds of faith, but they've sown the wrong kinds of seeds.

Brothers and sisters, we Christians have too much going for us to be walking, thinking, talking, and living in the negative all the time. We've got Jesus, and He has told us that if we have just a tiny bit of faith, we can move mountains for Him. All we have to do is take those positive seeds of faith—and I don't care how small they are—plant 'em, then stand back and watch 'em grow.

Right about now, you might be wondering how you go about planting those positive seeds. Maybe you're one of those people who have been farming the negative side for so long that you don't have the first idea of how to raise up a positive crop.

Well, it isn't always easy, but at the same time it's not as complicated as you might think.

UPGRADE OUR GARDENING TECHNIQUES

Some of the people in my church might find this hard to believe, but there are actually times when I don't feel like coming in to preach on Sunday mornings. There are mornings when I wake up feeling tired and unenthused and just don't want to get out of bed.

I can remember some early Sunday mornings when I just lay there and prayed, "Lord, I am so tired. I just don't want to get up now. Can't I just get someone else to do the preaching today?" But Jesus just wouldn't let me get away with not planting that mustard seed of faith. "Son," He told me, "just sit up, put your feet on the floor, and get out of bed. It's time to do some planting!"

When I obey and get my body out of bed, something amazing happens. The next thing I know, I'm on my way to church, have a big smile on my face, and I'm singing praises. I just can't wait to get to church and preach the Word of God. When I finally do make it to church, I still have that smile.

"Well, Hutch," you say, "that's all well and good, but how much faith does it take just to get out of bed?" If you're among those who are thinking that, then congratulations! You may have just stumbled onto the most important part of this teaching about mustard-seed faith.

See, planting a mustard seed of faith doesn't mean that you need a lot of faith. It simply means that you do those simple things God calls you to do, knowing that

He rewards people who have faith in Him.

But how can you start planting positive seeds of faith? You can start by doing some simple things like…

…rolling out of bed when God says to.

…keeping your appointment with God in your Bible reading and prayer times.

…responding to the Lord in obedience when you feel like procrastinating.

…believing in and acting on God's promises instead of focusing on your circumstances.

…resting in His care and control instead of complaining.

…trusting in the fact that God's got your back, and He will make something good out of even your worst situations.

…refusing to be angry and bitter at someone who has offended you—your spouse, your child, your boss, your estranged friend—and start praying for God's best for that person.

…putting a stop to worries about the future, choosing instead to thank God that He's working, sometimes behind the scenes, to bring you to that place in life He has for you.

…refusing to be intimidated by what people will

think of you, and start proclaiming the name of Jesus!

Now let me ask you, how much faith does it take to do simple things like these? Not much at all, really. These are things any of us Christians can do, even if we don't consider ourselves a "giant of the faith." They're all simple, tiny seeds of faith that we can plant, starting today! *And hear me, my friend, we have no idea—not the slightest inkling—of how God can use those simple acts of faith and obedience to shake up the world and impact eternity.*

In my case, instead of just lying around and being negative because I didn't feel like getting out of bed, I did something very simple: By just getting out of bed and doing what I've been called and prepared to do, I planted a small seed of faith. And because I did, God blessed me and the people He's put in my spiritual care.

It's incredible what God can do when we plant just a tiny little seed of faith. It amazes me how He can take that little seed—once it begins sending down its tiny roots—and make big changes in my life and in those around me.

A big God can shake the world through just a tiny particle of faith.

THE INFILTRATION SITUATION

Jesus told the disciples the Parable of the Mustard Seed, and in the very next breath He spoke yet another one of His spiritual stories, the Parable of Yeast. It goes like this: "The kingdom of heaven is like yeast that a woman took and mixed into a large amount of flour until it worked all through the dough" (Matthew 13:33, NIV).

When you read Matthew 13:31–33, you might well wonder just what in the world mustard seeds and yeast have to do with one another. What kind of recipe is that? Well, just hang with me and I'll show you!

In the Bible—other than in this parable—the word *yeast* or *leaven* is always used as a negative. Yeast was seen as a corrupting force, something that infiltrates the purity of something else, specifically simple obedience to God's Word. For example, Jesus Himself once told His disciples, "Take heed and beware of the leaven of the Pharisees and the Sadducees" (Matthew 16:6). In other words, He was telling them to be careful not to allow the corruption of the teaching of the religious leadership of that time to taint the simple truth of God's Word.

Just about everyone in our culture knows what yeast is good for: to make dough rise and expand so that the final product has an appealing texture and flavor. Yeast is actually a living organism. When exposed to the right amount of moisture and warmth, it gives off a gas that causes dough to rise and expand. That's why when a baker puts together a batch of dough and adds yeast it expands to twice its original size. Yeast does all this *invisibly*—you can see that it's working because the dough is rising, but you can't see or totally understand how.

Now what is the spiritual application here? What was Jesus saying when He compared the kingdom of heaven to yeast? He wanted His disciples to understand that while they may not have been able to see or understand how God worked through them, they could be assured that He was indeed doing the behind-the-scenes work it took to bring fruit out of their labors.

Now, how does this relate to "enough faith"?

Well, think back a minute to what I said earlier about planting a mustard-seed faith: that it can be for the positive and for the negative. While Jesus had at one time spoken of yeast being a corrupting force, He also wanted us to understand that a certain type of "yeast"—the yeast of faith—can influence and affect the world around us for the kingdom of God in the same way yeast affects dough.

In other words, it expands!

When we plant those seeds of faith—microscopic as they may be—we can rest assured that God Himself will make them grow. It will only be a matter of time before those seeds expand into something far bigger and more amazing than any of us could have imagined.

A GROWING, EXPANDING VISION

Now, let me go back for a minute to the story of William Wilberforce. I pointed out earlier how he planted a small seed of faith that grew into a widespread movement to stop the slave trade in the British Empire.

But it didn't stop there with the Brits.

Opposition to the horrible, immoral practice of slavery started to spread throughout the world—including the "New World"—and eventually the practice of the enslavement of Africans was outlawed throughout the world.

Wilberforce had helped bring about what the overwhelming majority of the people in the British Empire believed wasn't possible: the abolition of the slave trade. Do you see the pattern here? Plant a seed of faith—no matter how insignificant it may seem to you or anybody else—place your trust in the great and mighty God who can move mountains, and persevere, no matter how long it takes.

The results? Well, we can't even calculate how far and how wide God might send the branches of that "mustard tree" from our tiny mustard seed. It might cover the earth one day. It might reach down through time and touch generations yet unborn.

God plus one is always the majority—especially when that one steps out in faith, believing in Him to do something mighty.

The good news, my friend, is that you have all the faith you need.

2

ENOUGH FAITH
TO FOLLOW—CONSISTENTLY
AND PERSISTENTLY

Filled with accounts of Jesus performing spectacular miracles, Matthew 9 shows how He loves to work on behalf of people who simply come to Him in faith and expect Him to work.

How much faith do they demonstrate? Just enough to come to Jesus for answers to life's trials and problems.

In this chapter, we see Jesus raising the daughter of a religious leader from the dead, as well as healing a woman who had been suffering for twelve years with an internal hemorrhage (9:20). And we also see Him giving sight to two men who had just enough faith to do one thing: follow Him—consistently and persistently. Here's how Matthew told this short but very important story:

When Jesus departed from there, two blind men followed Him,
crying out and saying, "Son of David, have mercy on us!"
And when He had come into the house, the blind men came to
Him. And Jesus said to them, "Do you believe that I am able to
do this?" They said to Him, "Yes, Lord." Then He touched their
eyes, saying, "According to your faith let it be to you."
And their eyes were opened.

9:27-30

Man, I love this story! Here are two really needy guys who took what faith they had and laid it on the line—and who were willing to demonstrate that faith openly and in a way that many might not have had the nerve to do.

How much faith did they need to do that? How much faith did it take to bring their friend to Jesus?

I don't doubt that these blind men knew about what Jesus had already accomplished that day. You can bet they felt the stirring in the city that day, and heard all the whispers. They had heard that He had healed a woman who had been sick for twelve years and then raised a young girl from the dead. In fact, they had begun following Jesus around the moment He stepped out of Jairus's home. They were like so many others who believed Jesus could help them, just because they had seen—or at least heard about—some of His miraculous healings and deliverances.

What amazes me most about this account is the fact that these boys were so persistent in their request. Jesus had no sooner left the home of Jairus than they began following Him, yelling out, "Have mercy on us, Son of David!" They followed Jesus—not only just down the street, but into the very house where He was staying that night. They weren't worried about etiquette or their Sunday manners or about doing things properly. They couldn't have cared less about their public image or what others might say about them. They were worried about one thing and one thing only: getting God's attention.

This is something I don't want you to miss. Here we have two men in obvious need. And you would not have seen them sidling up to one of the disciples and meekly saying, "Listen, we don't want to be a bother, but when you get a chance could you ask Jesus for us to have a little mercy here, because we're both blind guys, and well, you know, it would really be helpful if He would just come over here and help us out a little."

No! They shouted out with loud voices. They

screamed, "HAVE MERCY ON US, SON OF DAVID!"

They were bold. They were brazen. They were socially incorrect. They were desperate.

And none of that offended Jesus a bit.

In fact, He responded to that flicker of faith He saw in their hearts and did for them exactly what they asked. That's an amazing display of a little bit of faith, isn't it? And it's the same kind of faith we need when we want God to move on our behalf.

HOW FAR ARE YOU WILLING TO GO?

Right now I'm going to meddle a little bit and ask you a question. When you are in need—when you are in a place where you absolutely need God to step into some area of your life—do you worry about showing good manners? Do you just quietly ask the deacons at your church to send up a well-worded, religious-sounding prayer for you? Do you rattle off some pious-sounding request making sure all the I's are dotted and all the T's crossed? Or do you do what these two blind men did, and just cry out to Him for His grace and His mercy with as loud a voice as you can muster?

I've come to the conclusion that too many Christians are more concerned about doing things "proper" than they are with persistently, fervently, and even loudly calling out to God and asking Him to meet their needs.

Now, I'm not saying you should go to your job and start yelling out "JESUS!" all the time and scaring people. I'm not talking about walking down the street, screaming out, "Have mercy on me, Son of David!" If you did that, someone driving a padded truck might pull up and take you away. I'm talking about not being worried in your prayer life about wording things just right or following the right protocol. I'm talking about being willing to shout out to God for the mercy you need in your present situation.

How much faith does it take to cry out to God for mercy?

There are times in all our lives when we're hurting so bad that we don't even know how to pray or what to say when we're doing it. Those are the times when we need to get on our faces and just let out the loudest cry we can to God. I'm not talking about being disrespectful. We always need to remember that He is our Lord and that we are here to serve Him. I'm talking about getting on our faces and crying out to our heavenly Father.

Why do we do that? Because God is hard of hearing or can't make out what we're saying because of all the background noise in the universe? ("Pipe down for a minute, all you angels, I think I hear a prayer from Seattle—might be Hutch!") Of course not. But the Lord responds to those who cast themselves upon His mercy and cry out to Him with all their hearts...even when their faith is "small."

In the psalms, David wrote: "I cry aloud to the LORD; I lift up my voice to the LORD for mercy. I pour out my complaint before him; before him I tell my trouble" (142:1–2, NIV). At the very beginning of this psalm we're told that David wrote these words "when he was in a cave." That would have been during those dark, frightening years when David was hounded across Israel by Saul, that jealous maniac of a king.

At the end of his rope, David cried aloud to God for help. Maybe he went back as far as he could into that dark cave and just shouted until he was hoarse. He pleaded with the Lord for protection and mercy, and that's just what the Lord gave him. Desperate as he was, David was in no mood for polite little "now-I-lay-me-down-to-sleep" prayers. In great need, he prayed with great intensity.

I have a friend whose wife was suffering with cancer. During his lunch hours, he started going way back into the pine forest at the edge of town and just yelling to God for mercy. He said he felt a little self-conscious about doing that at first. He'd been brought up as a proper Baptist, praying proper prayers. But once he started crying out loud to his heavenly Father, something clicked. The tears came, the emotions boiled over, and soon he felt just like a little child pulling on his Daddy's trousers, pleading for attention and help.

How much faith did my friend have? Enough faith to go into the woods during his lunch hours and cry aloud to God.

It was the same with the two blind men. They had come to a point where they were hurting so bad and in such serious need that they didn't care what anyone else thought about them calling out to Jesus—loudly and persistently. They didn't worry about breaches of etiquette and they didn't worry about disturbing Jesus. They just wanted His attention, and they were willing to do whatever it took to get it.

REMEMBER WHOM YOU'RE ASKING

It's sometimes easy when we read our Bibles to miss some of the important details in favor of seeing the bigger picture. In the story of the blind men following Jesus and begging for mercy, it's the bigger picture of two men who demonstrated what faith they had by calling out to Jesus in a socially unacceptable way.

But there are some details in this story I don't want you to miss.

First, I want you to note *where* this story is recorded: in the Gospel of Matthew—and the original target audience for that Gospel was first-century Jewish people. If you read Matthew from beginning to end, you'll probably notice a lot of references to Old Testament prophecies that Jesus fulfilled—more than sixty of them. These are things Jewish people would be able to understand more easily than most others.

The second thing I want you to catch is the way these two blind men addressed Jesus that day: "Have mercy on us, *Son of David*."

This is the first time in Matthew's Gospel that someone (other than the author) addressed Jesus that way (Matthew himself referred to Jesus as "the Son of David" in the very first verse of this book), and it's sure to get the attention of Jewish readers as well as those who were on the scene.

What's so important about Jesus being addressed as the Son of David? Because the Jewish people understood that their Messiah would be a descendant of King David. In that culture, the word *son* didn't apply just to the boy a man physically fathered, but also to his descendants. In other words, someone who was the great-great-great-great-grandson of King David would be referred to as his "son."

Later on in Matthew we see an exchange between Jesus and a bunch of Pharisees in which He asks them, "What do you think about the Christ? Whose Son is He?" These religious leaders answered the same way any devout Jew would: "The Son of David" (Matthew 22:41–42). These Pharisees weren't just quoting Jewish tradition. They knew that Old Testament prophecies about the Jewish Messiah promised that their Messiah would be a descendant of King David. That includes one prophecy found in the book of Jeremiah, written around 600 years before Jesus:

"The days are coming," declares the LORD, "when I will raise up
to David a righteous Branch, a King who will reign wisely and do
what is just and right in the land. In his days Judah will be
saved and Israel will live in safety. This is the name by which he
will be called: The LORD Our Righteousness."

23:5-6, NIV

When these two blind men called Jesus "Son of
David," they did something that might seem to us a
little out of place. When the Jewish people heard the
term "Son of David," they didn't think of mercy, but of
power. They were really hearing "Messiah," the One
God had promised, the One they had waited centuries
for, the One they believed would come and take over
and send the Roman legions packing. They were thinking about a conqueror and a military/political leader.

But when these blind men called out to Jesus for
mercy and addressed Him as "Son of David," it showed
two things. First, it showed they recognized their own
need and their own weakness. Second, and more
important, it showed they knew whom they were talking to and what He was capable of doing for them.
They weren't calling out to some weak, limited man,
but the Son of David, the One they knew had the God-

given authority to show them mercy that day.

These men understood something we all need to get hold of: In order to receive mercy, we need to go to someone who has the power to give it to us and the authority to make a difference!

I don't know about you, but when I have a huge need—say, healing for a life-threatening physical problem—I don't want to hear from some doctor who is lacking in knowledge and in the power to bring about the solution. Don't give me someone who cut his medical license from the back of a cereal box, give me someone who knows what he's talking about and has the ability to do something for me!

That is exactly what we have in Jesus Christ.

This is no paper tiger…no cardboard Messiah!

When we call out to Jesus for mercy, for healing, and for grace, we aren't calling on someone with weaknesses and limitations. We are calling on Someone who has the power and authority to overcome anything we have to endure and to bring us healing, peace, and forgiveness.

But what is our part when Jesus helps us in these ways? Just two things: Follow Him and believe He can do it! How much faith does *that* take?

THE IMPORTANCE OF FOLLOWING

Jesus had just left one house and was walking toward another when the men started shouting out to Him. Now you know that if at least one witness on the scene, Matthew, heard them, then Jesus had to have heard them, too. But He didn't turn around and give them what they asked for, or even acknowledge them. Instead, He just kept His sandals moving.

Why do you think Jesus seemed to be ignoring these boys? Why didn't He just turn around when they called on Him and tend to their need? For the very same reason it might seem He is ignoring us when we call out to Him: He wanted to know just how serious they were when it came to seeking a blessing from Him.

Why does Jesus wait to meet our needs some-times? He may want to test us. Are we seeking Him just because we're desperate, or because we have enough faith in Him and His power and authority? You see, Jesus already knows how serious we are when we cry out to Him, but sometimes He waits to move into our situations so that *we* can see how serious we are about running after Him and crying out to Him.

I wonder how many people have gone after Jesus, weeping in their desperation, only to turn to something or someone else when He didn't respond right away. I've seen both sides of that in my ministry. I've known people who have prayed literally for years knowing that God was going to meet their need, but also knowing that for reasons they couldn't understand He hadn't—at least in the timing and in the way they had asked Him to. On the other hand, I've known people who have cried out to God for a short time, only to give up and try something else when He didn't "perform" for them according to their timetable.

These two blind guys weren't about to give up. They followed Jesus from place to place, from house to house, all the while yelling out His name. Why? Because they knew that was the only way they were going to get what they needed.

Many times over, the Gospels tell us that Jesus challenged people to follow Him. Matthew tells us that Jesus called the brothers Simon Peter and Andrew, both fishermen by trade, to "*Follow Me*, and I will make you fishers of men" (4:19). Later, in the same Gospel, Jesus said to another of the disciples (one who wanted to first bury his father), "*Follow Me*, and let the dead bury their own dead" (8:22). Finally, there was the call of Matthew himself. Matthew was a tax collector for the Roman government, which meant that the Jewish people held him in very low esteem, but Jesus called him to "*Follow Me*" (9:9).

These men, and the rest of the Twelve, accepted Jesus' call to follow Him, and because they obeyed, they played a huge part in God's plan to bring salvation to the Jewish people and to the rest of the world. (Even Judas did that, when you think about it.)

Now how much faith do you think it took for them to simply follow Jesus? No more faith than it took for them to simply get up from where they were and start putting one foot in front of the other as they went where He went!

It doesn't take a lot of faith to take that first step of following Jesus or to continue following Him. *It's simply a matter of getting up from where we are and going where He's going.* And it's a matter of believing He can do whatever He tells us He can do on our behalf.

DO YOU BELIEVE I CAN DO IT?

Finally, after listening to the two blind men making a racket all the way down the street, Jesus acknowledged them. After they had broken every law of first-century etiquette, He spoke to them, but when He finally spoke, He asked them, "Do you believe that I am able to do this?" (Matthew 9:28).

That sounds like a silly question at first read, doesn't it? If someone had asked me that question after I'd followed him around for hours on end pleading for help, then I might get a little sarcastic. "Oh no, I don't believe You can do this," I might say. "That's why I've been following You around making a fool of myself and calling You the Son of David. *Of course I believe You can do it!*"

These two blind men had basically made fools of themselves, following Jesus around and crying out to Him. But they took their "foolishness" another step when they followed Him into the house where He was staying. Why did they risk that? Because they believed He could help them. And because they proved that they had enough faith, Jesus answered them.

The question we all need to answer is this: *Do we believe He is able to do it?* You see, it's not a matter of drumming up enough faith to get Him to do what we want Him to do. It's a matter of acting on that tiny bit of mustard-seed-sized faith that both pushes us to follow Him and assures us in our hearts that Jesus can do for us what He's promised.

The two blind men persistently followed Jesus, and in His perfect timing their persistence paid off. Jesus touched their eyes and told them, "According to your faith will it be done to you" (Matthew 9:29, NIV), and their sight was restored on the spot.

This is a beautiful verse that tells us a lot about faith, but it's also one of the worst-taught Scriptures in the whole Bible. Some believers have done God and His Word a great disservice by teaching that the size of God's blessings—physical as well as spiritual—are somehow dependent on the size of our faith. Or worse yet, many of them teach that we somehow have control over the difficulties God allows to come our way. If, for example, God allows cancer or some other terrible disease to invade our bodies, some believe that you just have to say in faith, "I don't receive that," and that's the end of it.

But that's *not* what Jesus was saying.

Not even close.

These two men didn't have a large amount of faith, but they put what faith they had into action by following Jesus until it was the right time for Him to respond to them. When He did, He had this message for them: "Boys, since you believe I can do this for you, then you have enough faith. Your blindness is over!"

WANTS OR NEEDS?

Matthew's account of these two blind men following Jesus drives home a theme we see throughout the Bible. Sometimes, God puts us in a place of genuine need to bring us to a point where we'll follow Him no matter what it costs us, no matter how foolish we may look, and no matter how long it takes.

If you're like me, you want the peace of God in your life—you like that part of it—but you'd rather not have to deal with being in a tough situation in order to receive it. You want the comfort of God but you don't want to be put in an uncomfortable situation. You want His healing, but you don't want to be sick.

If we're really honest with ourselves, we have to admit that none of us wants to be put in an impossible situation—one where we're sunk if God doesn't come through for us. We don't want to be in a situation physically where doctors and medicine can't help us. We don't want to be in a situation emotionally where no amount of counseling or therapy will do us any good. We don't want to be in a financial spot where there's nothing we can do to make enough money to pay off our bills.

But guess what? Those are exactly the kinds of situations—*impossible* situations—where God does His best work on our behalf.

I know I love having God's peace, but the truth is that sometimes I'm at peace just because everything's fine in my life. It's at those times when my fleshly thinking can convince me that I have God's peace and comfort. But I've learned that it's only when I'm in a place of need that I truly lean on God and receive those things from Him.

It's important that we see the difference between our needs and our wants. The biggest difference between the two? It is God who brings the *needs* into our lives, and He does that by allowing—or maybe even causing—circumstances that take us beyond our wisdom, skill, understanding, or endurance. On the other hand, our *wants* come from ourselves, because we desire more comfort, more money, or more fulfillment in the earthly or fleshly sense.

For example, if we want to continue living a life of faith—a life that tells everyone around us that we truly trust God to take care of us in the midst of a bad situation—we *need* His peace. And if we want to continue trusting God and believing that He really is the God of all comfort, we *need* to feel Him comforting us.

But there's another big difference between our needs and our wants, and it's this: God has promised to fulfill every one of our genuine needs. If we have a need that God Himself has allowed to come into our lives, He's sure to meet that need. On the other hand, if it's just a want, then we might not get it. In fact, I'd say we probably aren't going to get it.

WHEN WE DON'T RECEIVE

I hope I don't shock you when I say this, but I believe it's a solid biblical truth that when God doesn't answer our prayers the way we prayed them, we have a reason and a right to be upset and disappointed.

Now before you toss this book in the trash thinking I've bought into some of the worst teaching our cultural Christianity has to offer, I want you to bear with me and understand what I'm really saying. Here's what I mean: When God doesn't give us precisely what we asked for, we have a right to be put out—*not at God, but at ourselves.*

I say that because when God goes a different direction than what we prayed for, it's most often because we weren't walking with Him closely enough to know what to pray for in the first place. In other words, we weren't *following* Him like we should.

The apostle John gives us an incredible promise when it comes to prayer: "Now this is the confidence that we have in Him, that if we ask anything according to His will, He hears us. And if we know that He hears us, whatever we ask, we know that we have the petitions that we have asked of Him" (1 John 5:14–15).

A lot of Christians hear and receive John's words— "we know that we have what we asked of Him"—but somehow miss the most important part of this passage: "if we ask anything *according to His will.*"

Unfortunately, there is some unsound teaching out

there today that says that praying "according to God's will" somehow demonstrates a lack of faith on our part. But I believe that God put the instructions to pray "according to His will" in the Word because He wants us to actively and consistently follow Him and personally seek His will for all areas of our lives.

But how do we know what God's will for us really is? It's a matter of having enough faith to follow Jesus and walk in close fellowship with Him. It's a matter of seeking out His will in prayer, in His Word, and from wise, Spirit-filled counselors.

We serve an awesome God who wants more than anything to bless us and meet our every need. But there's a problem, and it's *our* problem: Too many of us pray for God to meet our needs and our wants, but we aren't in close enough fellowship with Him. We either harbor sin in our lives, or we neglect to do the very things that bring us more "in tune" with Him.

In Ephesians 5:10, Paul tells us, "Find out what pleases the Lord" (NIV).

Do you know what pleases the Lord when He looks down on your life? Have you spent enough time with Him to really learn the things that please or displease Him? Do you have any idea what *God* wants you to pray for and talk to Him about?

For example, how many of us have prayed for healing while neglecting to ask God for the grace and mercy—both of which are ironclad promises in the Bible—it takes to help us endure our physical pain? And how many of us, when we are faced with other difficulties, pray for deliverance but don't ask God for the wisdom (again, something the Bible promises us He will give us in abundance if we ask in faith) to know how to handle them appropriately?

Too many of us go to God in prayer only as a last resort! We've tried everything humanly possible to get what we need, and when all else fails, we go to our heavenly Father.

That's not the way God intended for us to live our lives in Him. He wants us to have a living, growing relationship with Him, the kind where we hear His voice and follow Him with everything we have. When that happens, He hears and answers our prayers according to His own perfect will.

It takes faith to do that, doesn't it?

The good news, my friend, is that you have all the faith you need.

3

ENOUGH FAITH
TO BE RENEWED

They were the most incredible words the crowd had ever heard. They listened intently, and with a deep sense of awe, as the Teacher declared principle after life-changing principle.

What was happening in their day? What was stirring? First, John the Baptizer stepped onto the scene, and now...the Galilean Rabbi. Miracles and wonders were in the air. They were hearing from God for the first time in four centuries—and it was startling. In many ways the new teaching was much more practical and easily applied than the Jewish law all of them had grown up reading and memorizing.

But in another sense it was more difficult to hear.

Responding to the Teacher's words would mean big changes in how they related to God and to one another.

The Jewish religious leadership of that day had done some things to God's Law He had never intended to be done, loading it down with an oppressive set of man-made rules and regulations. Because of that, the people had lost their freedom to worship and serve God in the way He had set forth and desired.

It was just that kind of rigid legalism that Jesus spoke out against and corrected as He delivered what we now call the Sermon on the Mount, recorded in Matthew 5–7. It was a message that turned the world of His day upside down. People couldn't believe what they were hearing! In that hillside message, He gave new teaching on a wide variety of topics concerning faith and Jewish law. (It wasn't really "new" as much as it was a fresh-from-heaven understanding of what God had desired all along.) It was a GPS reading that said, "You guys are way, way off the path. You're as lost as you can be, but follow Me, and I'll lead you back to heaven's true coordinates."

Many in the Jewish religious leadership had problems with Jesus' teaching, believing it contradicted or overruled the law of Moses. But that wasn't what Jesus was doing at all. In fact, He told the people listening to Him that day, "Do not think that I have come to abolish the Law or the Prophets; I have not come to abolish them but to fulfill them. I tell you the truth, until heaven and earth disappear, not the smallest letter, not the least stroke of a pen, will by any means disappear from the Law until everything is accomplished" (Matthew 5:17–18, NIV).

WHOSE LAW?

"But how can anyone say that Jesus never broke any of the Jewish laws?" you might be asking. "When you read the Gospels, it seems like every time Jesus opens His mouth He's offending the establishment by breaking some kind of law."

There's no question that Jesus offended the sensibilities of the Jewish religious leadership by being what they considered "too free" with His words and actions.

For example, the twelfth chapter of Matthew tells us that the Pharisees and other religious leaders got all bent out of shape when they saw Jesus' disciples walking through a field plucking grain and eating it. They didn't object to the disciples "gleaning" from another person's field—that was permissible under the Law—but took serious issue with the disciples doing the "work" of harvesting on the Sabbath. Later that very Sabbath, He upset the Pharisees even further by healing a man.

But the truth is Jesus never strayed one inch from perfect obedience to the law of God. He was simply redirecting the people's attention away from the phony man-made rules, traditions, and legalisms, which the people found all-but-impossible to keep anyway.

Jesus turned this religious world on its ear when He came on the scene and basically announced, "Things are going to change! The way you worship God and the way you serve your fellow man—all of it's going to change and change big-time!"

This wasn't an "out with the old, and in with the new" message.

It was a message of *renewal*.

And it was a message Jesus preached from a position of perfect obedience and perfect authority.

THE AUTHORITY OF JESUS TO RENEW

As we read through Matthew and the rest of the Gospels, we see that the Jewish religious leadership completely missed the heart of what Jesus was really teaching. Not so with those who followed Him and *really* listened. Matthew tells us, "When Jesus had ended these sayings…the people were astonished at His teaching, for He taught them as one having authority, and not as the scribes" (7:28–29).

In other words, it wasn't just *what* Jesus said that got people's attention—as important as that was—but *how* He said it.

There's something very powerful in someone speaking with authority, isn't there? It's like those old television commercials that told us, "When E. F. Hutton talks, people listen." Are you old enough to remember those ads? Some guy at an outside café table would say, "Well, my broker is E. F. Hutton, and he says…" And suddenly everything on the whole scene would go dead silent and everyone would lean toward the speaker, trying to catch those valuable words of financial authority.

I'm big on authority. If I have chest pains, I'm not going to go to a mechanic to find out what's wrong with my body. I'm going to check things out with a doctor. I want someone who knows more about bones and blood than spark plugs. I want someone who speaks from a position of authority as to what's wrong and what I need to do about it. And I know the doctor has that authority because he has the training and the experience it takes to be able to make a correct diagnosis and prescribe the correct treatment.

That illustrates why so many people followed Jesus—and why so many people in power opposed Him and wanted Him dead. Jesus spoke with authority well beyond that of the Pharisees, Sadducees, and the religious establishment. It wasn't just because He knew the Scriptures so well (which He did), but because the Father had given Him the authority to speak and act on His behalf.

That is exactly what Jesus was saying when He told a group of Pharisees, "When you lift up the Son of Man, then you will know that I am He, and that I do nothing of Myself; but as My Father taught Me, I speak these things. And He who sent Me is with Me. The

Father has not left Me alone, for I always do those things that please Him" (John 8:28–29).

DEMONSTRATIONS OF AUTHORITY

It's one thing to *say* you have authority—or even to have someone else say it—but it's another thing altogether to *demonstrate* that authority. That's exactly what Jesus did. Starting with chapter 8 of his Gospel, Matthew records how Jesus not only spoke with supreme authority, but also acted with authority. In that one chapter alone, we read how Jesus healed people of leprosy and other physical problems, calmed a violent storm over the Sea of Galilee, and cast some really nasty demons out of two men.

Jesus demonstrated unquestionable authority—authority over people, over sickness, over earthly elements, and over the spiritual realm. This was the authority to change things and to make alive that which had been dead.

It was, in other words, the authority to renew.

That's the same authority He has in our lives today. But it's even more than authority—it's power. This is the authority and the power to take what once was dead—spiritually dead—and make it alive again.

One of the things I think is missing in a lot of Christian teaching today is Jesus' authority and power to change our lives and to renew us. Too many believers see Jesus as the ticket to heaven, but don't understand His desire and His unlimited ability to transform our lives from the inside out—while we're still living in the here and now.

You have enough faith for that, my friend. Never doubt it. If you have enough faith to believe Jesus can reach down from heaven, snatch you out of a life bound for hell, and put you on a path to eternal life, you have all the faith you need. Even if it's only a microscopic seed of faith, it is ENOUGH to claim the renewing, revitalizing, life-changing power of Jesus this very moment! You don't need to scurry around trying to scrape up enough faith. You just need to plant the little faith you have—and then stand back!

It's a sad commentary on the state of the church today that our lives are so drab, down, and defeated that we don't draw people to us. If we're not living the renewed, joyous, victorious lives Christ intended for us, what difference are we making in this sad, broken world? Is it any wonder that so many in the world don't want anything to do with us…or with Jesus?

Too many believers today—and I'm talking about people who have verbally acknowledged Jesus Christ as their Lord and Savior—don't live or talk as though they're serving the One who has the authority over everything in their lives. Sure, they talk a good game of faith on Sunday mornings when they're surrounded by other believers. But when they're out there in the world the other six days of the week, they don't look or sound any different than the unbelievers all around them.

Where is the spark? Where is the freshness? Where is the sense of wonder? Where is the joy, flowing like "rivers of water" from the their inmost being? (John 7:38.)

Why do the actions and words of many Christians seem to mirror those of the world around them? I'd say it's because we have neglected to plant a seed of faith, and to believe God for fresh new workings in our heart of hearts. We're not claiming by faith the truth that Jesus has renewed us and will continue to renew us day by day for the rest of our lives.

That's a lesson Jesus took the opportunity to drive home during a discussion on fasting. As He did so many times, He took a simple subject and went miles deeper than anyone expected.

A HEAVENLY WEDDING CELEBRATION

Jesus' whole earthly ministry was for the purpose of finding and saving the lost and giving them new life. He said, "The thief comes only in order to steal and kill and destroy. I came that they may have and enjoy life, and have it in abundance (to the full, till it overflows)" (John 10:10, AMP). This was a ministry of renewal, a ministry in which He sought to bring people into a relationship of love and obedience to the Father.

Matthew records a scene where Jesus explained the amazing "newness" of what He had come to do:

> Then the disciples of John came to Him, saying, "Why do we and the Pharisees fast often, but Your disciples do not fast?" And Jesus said to them, "Can the friends of the bridegroom mourn as long as the bridegroom is with them? But the days will come when the bridegroom will be taken away from them, and then they will fast. No one puts a piece of unshrunk cloth on an old garment; for the patch pulls away from the garment, and the

> tear is made worse. Nor do people put new wine into old wineskins, or else the wineskins break, the wine is spilled, and the wineskins are ruined. But they put new wine into new wineskins, and both are preserved."
>
> 9:14-17

Who was asking the questions here? It wasn't the Pharisees or any other Jewish religious leaders. This time it was the disciples of John the Baptizer, the one God had sent to prepare the Jewish world for Jesus' arrival in the first place. They had an honest question for Jesus that day, a question He was more than ready and willing to answer.

Jesus answered these men's concerns using something almost any Jewish person would have understood: a wedding celebration. Jewish weddings at that time were big parties, with food and drink everywhere. And in that culture, it would have been a major social faux pas and a slap in the face to the bride and groom and their families to fast during the wedding celebration.

When Jesus spoke of the wedding party, John's disciples knew He was referring to Himself as the long-awaited bridegroom and to His disciples as the guests. He was simply reminding them that He was the Messiah God had promised for centuries through the Old Testament prophets, and that while He was on earth with them it was time to celebrate, not time to fast.

Jesus didn't want His disciples behaving like so many others of that time. He didn't want them fasting with a long face (a common practice during times of mourning over sin in the Jewish culture). Why should they fast, why should they be sad, why should they be down in the mouth or blue when *the Messiah* was in their midst? It was a time for celebration and joy, not mourning and strict self-denial.

Jesus wasn't downplaying the importance of the spiritual exercise of fasting. He wasn't saying believers shouldn't fast. On the contrary, He said that after He was gone the disciples would continue in the practice of fasting. (Also, remember what Jesus did right after His baptism? He went out to the wilderness for forty days, where He prayed…and fasted.)

Now what is the application for believers today? Jesus wants us to know that if we have Him living within us, there is no way we should be like the rest of the world, no way we should be down and upset, sour and miserable, no way we should live depressed, lack-luster lives—even when we're in the midst of difficulty or disappointment. We have *Jesus* with us. We're filled with His Holy Spirit. We have wide-open access to the Father. We've been set free from sin to serve Him. It's time to celebrate!

If you've read the other three Gospels, you know that Jesus didn't just leave His disciples—or us—hanging in space when He returned to the Father. John 16 tells us that before His death and resurrection, Jesus promised His followers that He would send them the Holy Spirit to be their Companion, Comforter, Counselor, and Friend. John 14 says, "And I will pray the Father, and He will give you another Helper, that He may abide with you forever, even the Spirit of truth, whom the world cannot receive, because it neither sees Him nor knows Him; but you know Him, for He dwells with you and will be in you" (v. 16–17).

Anyone who has accepted Jesus Christ as their personal Lord and Savior has God's Holy Spirit living within them…and that makes for a whole new ball game. No longer do we have to walk around worried or stressed or miserable. Why? Because we have *God Himself* inside us—closer than hands or feet, closer than breathing. He's available 24/7 to comfort us, direct us, and free us from the bondage of sin. In other words, *renew* us.

NEW PATCHES AND NEW WINE

Jesus answered John's disciples' question about fasting by first pointing out that while He was with them, they would celebrate by eating and drinking. But then He goes on to point out some common-sense truths concerning new patches and new wine.

No doubt the disciples of John were well aware that it's not a good idea to put an unshrunk patch on an old garment. I know my wife knows better than to patch an old pair of jeans with a new piece of denim. She knows that when you wash and dry that patched pair of pants, the new patch is going to shrink and make an even worse mess out of those jeans. At best, the patch is going to end up looking wrinkly and ugly, and the jeans will look worse than when they were holey!

They also understood that putting new wine in an old wineskin wouldn't work because old wineskins had lost their elasticity, and couldn't expand as the new wine fermented and became older wine. When that happened, the wineskin would burst and you would lose the wine and ruin an old but perfectly good wineskin.

What does that have to do with fasting or not fasting?

Jesus was reminding John's disciples that God had sent their own teacher to prepare the way for the Messiah, and to call the Jewish people to repent from a religious way of life so corrupted by human tradition that it barely resembled the way of life and worship that God had set up through His Word.

But He was also pointing out that He hadn't come to "patch up" the old system or to add His own teaching to it, but to replace it with something new. Jesus wanted John's disciples to understand that the old ways were finished and that all the human tradition and legalism were going to be a thing of the past. Instead, people were going to start enjoying God and celebrating their personal relationship with Him. That was going to start with the disciples, who weren't going to be taking part in any religious fasts while Jesus was with them.

This is a message of renewal and freedom in and through Jesus Christ, and it's a message all of us—as the body of Christ and as individuals—need to understand and apply today!

THE PROBLEM WITH OLD WINESKINS

Remember those big fuzzy dice people used to hang on their rearview mirrors? You can still spot them now and then on a restored '57 Chevy, or maybe a customized '68 GTO.

But fuzzy dice would never work in a Ferrari.

Something that tacky wouldn't fit in the interior of such a fine automobile. It would be out of place, wouldn't it? An embarrassment. It would be like a beautiful woman—dressed to the hilt in a gorgeous gown—wearing a pair of muddy logging boots.

Some things just don't belong together.

The very same thing is true of you and me when we hang on to our old ways after we've accepted Jesus Christ as our Lord and Savior. It just doesn't fit! We can't come to Jesus and then say, "I'm just gonna hang on to this one sin, because God knows I have needs and weaknesses, and He'll understand if I keep this one little sin around for a while."

That's like trying to pour the new wine of the Holy Spirit and renewal in Christ into the old wineskin of our willful, sinful behavior. It just won't work! Something's got to give! We will be weak Christians who are ineffective in our witness to an outside world that needs Jesus.

As a believer and follower of Jesus, you're supposed to walk away from your old life, away from the sinful ways and destructive habits of your life before you met Jesus. But too many believers try to keep a grip on some of those old "God-substitutes" they used to rely on in their pre-Christ days.

I once met a young man who came to me for counseling about the sin that had kept him in bondage: lust. He hadn't been a Christian very long, and so far he wasn't having the victory God has promised all of us over his past life. When he came to me, he said, "I just have the worst time in the world with lust. I can't seem to shake the constant thoughts about sex."

Well, I had a chance to visit this young guy at his home. What I saw showed me why he was fighting such a losing battle with lust. All over his bedroom were Playboy pinups. "Son," I said, "if I don't get out of here, *I* will be the one having a problem with lust."

Is it any wonder that this young man couldn't find release from these dark thoughts? I got out of there as quickly as I could, then told my young friend very firmly and very directly that he would never have the victory he wanted over the sin of lust until he got rid of all those pictures on his wall.

Too many believers who struggle with sin—in their actions and in their thoughts—are too quick to point to the works of the devil or demonic forces as the reason for their lack of victory. The devil wants more than anything to keep the child of God in bondage to sin, and he *can* use spiritual forces to achieve that end. While those things can be very real in the life of a believer, I'd be willing to bet that if you were to take a look at the life of a believer who is fighting a losing battle with sin, you'd see that it's because that person hasn't made the choice to remove the things that can so easily cause them to stumble.

Let me ask you some practical questions. If you were trying to kick an addiction to alcohol or drugs, would it make sense for you to keep a bottle in your cupboard or a stash in your glove box? If you're trying to stop living a life of sexual immorality, would it make sense to keep a box of dirty magazines and DVDs hidden away where only you knew where they were? And if you're trying to leave a life of occult practices, would it make sense to keep the old books and implements you used for those practices in your home?

Of course not! That would make about as much sense as going to the doctor after a lifesaving appendix operation and asking him to put that dirty, poison-ridden, and useless organ back in your belly.

You see, God didn't send Jesus to give you freedom and deliverance just so you could go right back into your old ways. He wants you to be free—completely free—and being completely free means making a decision to rid your life of the things that will tempt you into reverting back to your old ways.

Jesus came to earth and lived and died so that we could have freedom *from* the old ways and freedom *in* the new. And when we demonstrate enough faith to leave behind the old and embrace the new, we'll walk in the abundant freedom and life He came to bring us.

You have the faith to embrace this freedom. Don't let Satan or anyone else tell you otherwise!

The fact is, my friend, you have all the faith you need.

4

ENOUGH FAITH
TO WALK IN
JESUS' AUTHORITY

In his very last Sunday sermon before his murder in Memphis, Tennessee, on April 4, 1968, Dr. Martin Luther King said, "On some positions, cowardice asks the question, is it expedient? And then expedience comes along and asks the question, is it politic? Vanity asks the question, is it popular? Conscience asks the question, is it right?"

Dr. King was saying with great strength and conviction that doing what is right is always right, even when it requires courage to do it, even when it isn't convenient, even when it isn't "politically correct" (whatever that means at a given time and place), and even when it isn't the popular thing to do.

That is the same call God has given His church today. It's a call to walk in courage and integrity as we take the message of the gospel of Jesus Christ to a world that desperately needs to hear it—but in most cases wishes we'd keep our mouths shut about God.

Sadly, however, too many of us aren't answering that call.

I become more amazed, more saddened, and more frustrated every day as I recognize how far the church has drifted from faith and obedience to the Word of God, how far we've drifted from being the kind of church He wants us to be. And because we've drifted, the church has become weak in its witness to the outside world, ineffective in impacting our culture for God, and nearly powerless in battling the devil and his minions.

But I'll tell you what saddens and frustrates me most: We as a church and as individual believers have access to the most awesome power in the universe, and most of us don't even know it. And even if some of us *do* know it, we don't know how to access it and use it to do the things God calls us to do—things we could never do apart from Jesus Christ.

And what is the power I'm talking about? It's the authority of Jesus Christ over all things, the very same authority He has given those who have enough faith to access it and make it part of their daily walks with Him.

UNLIKELY CANDIDATES

Jesus began His public ministry following His baptism and temptation by the devil in the desert. As He began preaching and teaching, He attracted a large crowd of followers, people the Bible refers to as His disciples. In the Bible, the word *disciple* refers to one who learns from another person—in this case from Jesus.

The Gospels don't tell us how many disciples Jesus had, but it's likely—even probable—they numbered into the hundreds. But out of that larger group Jesus chose twelve men who would be His closest and most important followers, the men who were "called" to something more than simply following Jesus.

The first three Gospels—Matthew, Mark, and Luke—tell the story of who these men were, and how Jesus "ordained" them. Here is how Matthew tells the account:

> And when He had called His twelve disciples to Him, He gave them power over unclean spirits, to cast them out, and to heal all kinds of sickness and all kinds of disease. Now the names of the twelve apostles are these: first, Simon, who is called Peter, and Andrew his brother; James the son of Zebedee, and John his brother; Philip and Bartholomew; Thomas and Matthew the tax collector; James the son of Alphaeus, and Lebbaeus, whose surname was Thaddaeus; Simon the Cananite, and Judas Iscariot, who also betrayed Him.
>
> 10:1-4

There's something very important in these verses that might escape your notice in the first reading. Notice that verse 1 says, "He called his twelve *disciples*," and verse 2 tells us, "These are the names of the *twelve* apostles…"

The word *apostle* means "one sent by another" or "ambassador," and that is the role these twelve men would play in the ministry of Jesus Christ. They were the guys who would travel everywhere with Jesus, seeing Him doing things the others couldn't see and hearing Him teach things the others couldn't hear. And after Jesus was gone, they would be charged with the responsibility of taking His message into the world around them.

But what kind of men were they?

I can't speak for other people, but if I were choosing twelve men to start something as big as the church of Jesus Christ, I definitely wouldn't pick some of these guys. Most or all of them had personal résumés that were, to put it kindly, unimpressive. If a personnel agency presented me with these guys as their finalists, I'd fire the agency.

First there was Peter, a simple fisherman by trade. Peter meant well, but seemed to have a talent for saying and doing the wrong things at all the wrong times. Whenever I read about Peter in the Gospels, it seems that the only time he opens his mouth is to change feet.

Then there are James and John, the sons of Zebedee, who were also fishermen. Not only did these two seem more concerned with their own positions in Christ's kingdom, but they were also mama's boys. Mark's Gospel tells us that one day these two brothers approached Jesus and asked Him if they could sit on either side of Him on His throne of glory. Matthew's account of this scene is a little more detailed and tells us that it was actually their *mother* who made the request. Jesus' response? "You don't know what you're asking" (Mark 10:38, NIV).

Of course, most of us know Thomas for one thing: doubt. "Doubting Thomas" was the eternal pessimist of the group, and always seemed to have a complaint on his lips.

If there was one of these guys whom you'd think Jesus would have immediately marked off His list of candidates, it would probably be Matthew. By trade, he was a tax collector, which in those days made him a few notches lower than a scoundrel. In the eyes of almost all the Jewish people, tax collectors were nothing more than traitors, because they worked for the hated Roman government and padded their pockets by ripping off their own people.

Simon, the one the Bible calls "the Zealot," didn't look like a very likely candidate, either. The Zealots were the libertarians or separatists of first-century Judaism. Deeply resentful of the Roman government, these guys were willing to do anything it took—including murder and acts of terrorism against Romans and Jews alike—to throw off the rule of Rome. Before Jesus called my man Simon, he was a part of that violent, dangerous sect.

SO WHY THESE GUYS?

I can't help but think that some of Jesus' more "elite" followers were a little put off by His choice in apostles. I can almost hear them asking, "Out of all the people who follow Jesus, why would He pick *these* losers?"

Four fishermen. A crooked IRS agent. A doubter. A bomb-throwing radical. Certainly there had to be better candidates around than that! Maybe some people with more education and more credentials, and certainly some who had lived better lives than the scoundrel named Matthew or the fire-breather named Simon.

Jesus certainly didn't choose the most gifted or those with the best credentials. Instead, He chose ordinary, average men who had their own personal weaknesses as well as some skeletons in their closets. In other words, He chose people that look a lot like you and me!

Why do you suppose Jesus would pick men like these when there were probably more qualified people with better credentials among His followers? It would be like the president of the United States going down to the local manufacturing plant and picking twelve uneducated—and extremely flawed—people to be in his Cabinet. What's more, this wasn't some temporal world government Jesus was staffing; it was His very own earthly ministry, which would reach all the way through time into eternity!

I believe Jesus chose these twelve men because He looked into their futures and saw what they *could* be instead of what they were or had been. I believe that He chose them knowing their weaknesses, limitations, and pasts. He knew they would be teachable, and when controlled and empowered by His Spirit, would be the kind of men who could do great things for His kingdom.

But that would only happen consistently after they learned some things about the authority of their Teacher and Master.

WATCHING AND DOING

These chosen Twelve had traveled along with the other disciples and had seen Jesus do some mind-blowing miracles. They'd seen Him raise the dead, calm violent storms with a word, heal every kind of sickness, send demons running, create meals for thousands out of thin air, and teach with authority like they'd never seen before. Jesus had invited them to witness these things for one reason: so that they would know He had authority from heaven.

That was amazing enough. But then He took that amazement up to a whole new level. He told them they had the same authority, and could accomplish those same things—and even more!

Jesus didn't, as the saying goes, blow any sunshine up their skirts, either. He warned them that theirs wouldn't be an easy mission, that they would face opposition and persecution, that they might even face arrest and prosecution because they were preaching and healing in His name. He told them that their message wouldn't bring peace but that it would divide people, friends, and families. But He also sent them away with these words of encouragement:

> "And do not fear those who kill the body but cannot kill the soul. But rather fear Him who is able to destroy both soul and body in hell. Are not two sparrows sold for a copper coin? And not one of them falls to the ground apart from your Father's will. But the very hairs of your head are all numbered. Do not fear therefore; you are of more value than many sparrows."
>
> MATTHEW 10:28-31

Now what do you think was going through the apostles' minds when they heard Jesus say that? Were they wondering if they'd really be able to do those things, or did they have a "bring it on" attitude? Did they focus on the amazing things Jesus said they would do, or did they keep their eyes on the fact that God would care for them when things got tough? The Bible doesn't record any questions or responses on the part of the disciples, only that they went out as Jesus had commanded them.

Matthew doesn't give us any specifics about the results of the apostles' first missionary trip, only that as they went out Jesus began preaching and teaching in His home district of Galilee. But Mark and Luke both tell us that their trip was a slam-dunk success. Mark, who also pointed out that Jesus sent them out two-by-two, tells us "they went out and preached that people should repent. And they cast out many demons, and anointed with oil many who were sick, and healed them" (6:12–13).

Luke tells us essentially the same thing, but he also records what the Twelve did when they returned to Jesus: "And the apostles, when they had returned, told Him all that they had done" (9:10).

Now it's hard for me to imagine the apostles telling Jesus what happened as if they were giving an end-of-the-quarter financial report. I can't help but think that these guys were sky-high when they returned from a trip where they did the very same things Jesus Himself had been doing in front of them. I know if I'd just gotten back from a trip where I was seeing folks saved, healed, and delivered from demons in Jesus' name, I'd be on such a high that I'd start my prayers with "As long as I'm here…." I'd be thinking there's nothing I couldn't do for Jesus—and all because I had received authority from Him.

I don't doubt for a minute that that's how the apostles felt and talked when they returned to Jesus. But it didn't last—at least in the short run. Later on in the Gospel of Matthew, we read an account where they didn't act with the authority Jesus had given them.

"HOW LONG SHALL I PUT UP WITH YOU?"

In my prologue to this book, I wrote briefly about Matthew 17. This chapter tells the story a young boy in desperate need of healing, but whose demonic possession turned out to be more than nine of Jesus' disciples could handle.

Jesus had taken Peter, James, and John—His three closest disciples—to witness His "transfiguration," the event where the three saw Jesus in His full glory. But while they were on top of the mountain, Mark's Gospel tells us that a noisy and contentious scene broke out down below.

When Jesus and the three companions returned to the foot of the mountain, they were greeted by a man who had brought his demon-possessed son to the disciples for healing. The nine had tried to cast out the demon, but no dice. The poor kid was just as tormented and in peril as before. When this dad saw Jesus, he ran to Him, fell on his face, and begged Him, "Lord, have mercy on my son. He has seizures and is suffering greatly. He often falls into the fire or into the water. I brought him to your disciples, but they could not heal him" (Matthew 17:15–16, NIV).

Jesus sounded more than a little ticked off that the disciples were unable to heal the boy, and His angry response to their failure showed in His words: "O faithless and perverse generation, how long shall I be with you? How long shall I bear with you?" (v. 17). Another version of the Bible catches what Jesus was saying a little better: "You stubborn, faithless people! How long must I be with you until you believe? How long must I put up with you?" (NLT).

What went wrong when the disciples tried to heal this demon-possessed boy?

The disciples were wondering that same thing themselves.

WHAT WENT WRONG?

Later on, after Jesus had healed the boy and sent him and his father on their way, the disciples went to Him in private and asked Him the question of the day: "Why couldn't we drive it out?" Jesus gave a very telling response when He told them, "Because of your unbelief; for assuredly, I say to you, *if you have faith as a mustard seed*, you will say to this mountain, 'Move from here to there,' and it will move; and nothing will be impossible for you" (v. 20, italics added).

What Jesus wanted the disciples—and us today—to understand was that it wasn't a matter of *how much* faith they possessed, but where they *put* the faith they had. The disciples apparently had failed to cast out that demon because they hadn't done it through faith in Christ. Instead, they tried to do it on their own. They had taken their eyes off of the thing Jesus had given them to deal with sickness and evil spirits: authority. And when they did that, the results were the same for them as they are for us when we try to do things without faith: They fell flat on their faces.

PREACHING, TEACHING, AND LIVING WITH AUTHORITY

Earlier, I told you some things about some of the disciples, things that might make us wonder just what Jesus was thinking when He picked these guys. Now I want to tell you about what a bunch of ordinary—sometimes less than ordinary—men did because they had enough faith to believe in Jesus and in His authority to do the things He told them to do.

After Jesus' resurrection and before His ascension back to heaven, He charged the disciples with what is called "the great commission":

"All authority has been given to Me in heaven and on earth. Go therefore and make disciples of all the nations, baptizing them in the name of the Father and of the Son and of the Holy Spirit, teaching them to observe all things that I have commanded you; and lo, I am with you always, even to the end of the age."

MATTHEW 28:18-20

That's exactly what they did, too!

By now you know that Simon Peter was the man God used to get this whole Christianity thing rolling. Even though he had shown himself to be impulsive and prone to stumbling around, he spent the remainder of his life after Jesus had left speaking out with incredible courage and authority, as he took the message of Jesus to the Jewish world. Peter did this in the face of incredible persecution from the Jews and the Roman authorities.

All of that from a man who had been so overtaken with fear that he abandoned Jesus as He was about to be tried and executed!

But Peter wasn't the only one of the remaining eleven original apostles who made a difference for the kingdom of God.

Of the original twelve, John was the only one not

to die a violent death, although he did face his share of persecution. Just before the destruction of Jerusalem by the Romans in 70 AD, John moved to Ephesus, where he became the pastor of the Ephesian church. Before his death in around 99 AD, John had not only led the Ephesian church through some horrendous times, but had also written the Gospel that bears his name—as well as the book of Revelation.

Although the eventual fates of the remaining apostles aren't recorded in the Bible, history and Christian tradition hold that they all made their marks for Christ preaching in places such as Egypt, Asia Minor (now Turkey), Persia, Ethiopia, Assyria, and out to the frontiers of the known world.

The apostles had gone from being strong and authoritative Matthew 10 believers to being weak Matthew 17 Christians. But because they had seen and heard for themselves the things that Jesus did—including raising people from the dead—and believed that He had all authority over everything in heaven and earth, they became something more than they ever were when He was with them. They became book-of-Acts Christians, the kind of Christians who turned their worlds upside down for Him.

SO WHAT HAS HAPPENED SINCE?

Take the time to read the book of Acts and you'll see some very ordinary people doing extraordinary things for the kingdom of God. You'll see people boldly and bravely preaching the name of Jesus Christ to a world that desperately needed Him, but which was often violently hostile to His message.

In other words, you'll see the stories of people who lived as though they really believed in the power and authority of the Lord Jesus Christ. And because they had that kind of faith, they got to *see* that power and authority in action.

Now, fast-forward almost two thousand years and look at our church today. You'll see a sad picture of people living lives of fear instead of boldness, bondage instead of freedom, and defeat instead of victory in Jesus Christ. You'll see a church that doesn't attract people, simply because it doesn't have anything to offer a world that still needs Jesus.

I believe this is because many of us today don't truly understand what it means to live and walk in the authority of Jesus Christ. And when believers don't understand the authority of Jesus, there is no way they can do the things He calls them to do in order to further His kingdom.

I want my whole life and my whole ministry to be built around the power and authority of Jesus Christ. If I don't do this—if this doesn't happen—what do I have? *I have nothing!* Nothing but a sham, and there's already enough of that to go around! While looking at those miraculous things Jesus called the apostles to do through His authority, I want to have a personal attitude that says, "Why not now?" And I want Antioch Bible Church in Kirkland, Washington, to be an example of what a local body can do when it is sold out to believing wholeheartedly in the authority of Christ. I know that as that happens, lives will be changed. Folks will be coming to Jesus for the first time, and those who know Him already will begin seeing Him do amazing things in their lives.

What does it take for that to happen? What does it take for it to happen in your church and in your personal walk? It takes ordinary people like you and me having just a little faith in a Savior who has taught us and empowered us to live under His authority and power.

Let me say it again (and I'll say it several more

times, too): It's not how much faith you possess, or how "big" your faith might be that matters. And it's not your credentials that matter, either. What matters is knowing about the authority you have in Jesus Christ and then putting that authority into action.

Go forward with confidence, my brother, my sister, because you have all the faith you need.

5

ENOUGH FAITH
TO FREELY GIVE

Jesus Christ changed lives wherever He went. If He wasn't casting out demons, raising the dead, and healing the sick, then He was giving profound, life-changing teaching.

Jesus was, to use a sports cliché, a "difference maker" in the world, and He called His disciples to be difference makers, too.

That's the same call He gives each and every one of us who know Him today.

Jesus made a difference in the world because He freely gave of everything the Father had given Him. And because He is still busy freely giving today—but now from a position at the Father's right hand—we as His followers have the power to make a difference in the world around us here and now.

THE CALL TO FREELY GIVE

In the last chapter, I wrote about how Jesus had chosen twelve ordinary, average men and given them authority over demons and over physical sickness.

Jesus began His instructions for the Twelve this way:

> "Do not go among the Gentiles or enter any town of the Samaritans. Go rather to the lost sheep of Israel. As you go, preach this message: 'The kingdom of heaven is near.' Heal the sick, raise the dead, cleanse those who have leprosy, drive out demons. Freely you have received, freely give."
>
> MATTHEW 10:5-8, NIV

Can you imagine growing up in a family where being bigoted and prejudiced against people who were different from you had become accepted tradition? Can you imagine having the idea drilled into you from birth that people who looked different from you or talked different from you were somehow not as good as you? Well, that is exactly the kind of families the disciples had grown up in. It was what they knew, what they'd always practiced.

In the eyes of the typical Jew in first-century Palestine, Gentiles (non-Jews) were seen as less than human—absolute heathens who weren't even good enough to talk to, let alone associate with. And maybe one step below the Gentiles in the eyes of Jewish people at that time were the Samaritans. They were mixed-race descendants of Jewish people who had intermarried with Assyrian colonists starting in the eighth century BC. The Jewish people hated the Samaritans so bitterly that when those in Galilee traveled to Jerusalem for the yearly feasts, such as Passover, they would travel around Samaria rather than take the much shorter route directly through Samaria.

These were the people Jesus specifically told the disciples to avoid as He sent them out.

We know this is a "for-now" command, first because the Gospels tell us that Jesus went through Samaria Himself and had even done the unthinkable for a Jewish rabbi: talking and ministering to a Samaritan woman (John 4:1–42). Second, we know that the message of salvation through Jesus Christ would later be taken to the Gentile world, largely through the work of the apostle Paul, who Jesus Himself said was "a chosen vessel of Mine to bear My

name before Gentiles, kings, and the children of Israel"
(Acts 9:15).

All of this was in keeping with a couple of Old
Testament prophecies—as far back as the book of
Genesis—concerning the fact that the Messiah's mission was not just to the Jews but also to the Gentile
world. "And the LORD said, 'Shall I hide from Abraham
what I am doing, since Abraham shall surely become a
great and mighty nation, and *all the nations of the earth
shall be blessed in him?*'" (Genesis 18:17–18, italics
added).

Now if Jesus came to save both Jew and Gentile,
and if He had come to be a blessing to "all nations,"
why did He tell the disciples to minister to the Jewish
people only? Is it because He, like His fellow Jews,
believed that His people were somehow better than
non-Jews?

Absolutely not! Jesus knew what His mission on
earth was, and He understood that He had come as the
Savior of all people, starting with the Jews but including all humankind. In other words, the Jews, as the
people God had chosen to bring the Messiah into the
world, would have the first opportunity to accept their
Messiah.

That is what the apostle Paul was talking about when he wrote, "For I am not ashamed of the gospel of Christ, for it is the power of God to salvation for everyone who believes, for the Jew first and also for the Greek" (Romans 1:16).

Jesus' message—the same one He commanded His disciples (and us), to take with them—was that things were about to change. He wanted them to tell the people that the time had come for a New Covenant, a new approach to the Law, and a new approach to worshiping God.

OUR HIGHEST MOTIVE

A lot of Christians today talk about their love for Israel. I love Israel myself, but I want to let you in on something: Jesus never said to *just* love Israel. He also said, "Go rather to the lost sheep of Israel. As you go, preach this message: 'The kingdom of heaven is near'"(Matthew 10:6, NIV).

I know a lot of people in this "politically correct" world have a real problem with Christians wanting to see the people of Israel come to faith in Jesus Christ.

But our bottom-line motivation for loving *all* people is to see them come to Christ for salvation. That includes the Jewish people, the race God used to bring Jesus into the world, and the race Jesus commanded the disciples to reach during their first missionary journey.

We are to love all people, regardless of skin color, ethnicity, nationality, or religion, and we are to do everything we can to make sure they have a chance to respond to Jesus' message of salvation.

I've heard a lot of missionaries who are devoted to reaching a certain culture for Jesus say things like, "I love the Chinese people" or "I love the Indian people," believing that their motivation for serving in those cultures should be their love for that particular people. But as shocking as this may sound, loving people—as individuals and as ethnic groups—isn't the right reason for us to go to reach them for Christ.

Our primary motivation for ministering to anyone should come out of our love for Jesus first and for the people second. Yes, we love these people with God's love—the kind of love that wants to see them saved—but we are to love Jesus even more.

In short, we are to "give" out of a pure desire to obey His command to do so.

When we make our love for Jesus our primary motivation for serving, we can serve with pure hearts, hearts that will reach out to the lost no matter what they do to us and no matter what they say to us. Only then are we freed to love even those who are unlovable—even those who do things to hurt us and reject us—just as Jesus loved a world that rejected Him and sentenced Him to death.

LOVING ENOUGH TO WANT THEM TO CHANGE

The principle each of us should take from Jesus' command to "give" is that we aren't just to go out and minister to people so that they can be healed, fed, clothed, and housed. We are also to give them the message that God wants to change their lives through Jesus Christ. As Christians, God calls us to love people just the way they are, which is the way *we* once were: lost and in need of the Savior. But He also calls us to love people in a way that gives them a chance to be changed.

It's a wonderful experience to feed the hungry, heal

the sick, and pray against demonic forces. I know that myself from some unforgettable personal experiences through the years. Those are all loving, Christlike things to do. But are we showing genuine, godly love if we meet people's physical needs, but allow those in need of salvation through Jesus Christ to remain lost and on the way to hell?

Just as Jesus sent His disciples to the "lost sheep of Israel," He now sends us to the lost sheep in our own world today. As we reach out to the lost, we are to give and meet their physical and emotional needs, but we aren't supposed to just stop there. We need to make sure that each and every one of the people we reach in Jesus' name understands that His kingdom is at hand, and that they need to make changes in their hearts and lives if they want to see that kingdom.

PREACH THE MESSAGE, BUT AS YOU DO...

Now in addition to preaching that the kingdom of heaven was at hand, Jesus commanded His disciples to, "Heal the sick, raise the dead, cleanse those who have leprosy, drive out demons" (Matthew 10:8, NIV).

Jesus sent out the disciples with the power and authority to do the very same things they had seen Him doing. Jesus had preached and taught, but He also healed the sick, raised the dead, cleansed lepers, and freed people of demons. Now the disciples, who were eyewitnesses of how to do these things perfectly, were going to follow in the footsteps of their Lord and do those same things.

But why do you suppose that Jesus gave the disciples these instructions? Why didn't He tell them to just verbally preach? Why didn't He just send them out with the "turn or burn" message? Well, there are a couple of reasons for that. Jesus understood that in order to prove to the Jewish people of that time and culture that He was who He claimed to be, it was necessary to demonstrate some power. That is what Paul was talking about when He wrote, "Jews demand miraculous signs and Greeks look for wisdom" (1 Corinthians 1:22, NIV).

These, then, are some practical instructions and teachings Jesus is giving here.

When individuals, churches, and other Christian ministries do "social work" such as adoption, crisis pregnancy counseling, drug and alcohol treatment, and clothing and feeding the needy, what do you think we are doing? We are meeting the physical and emotional needs of people so that they will be more open to having their spiritual needs met.

As individuals and as groups who want to reach people for Jesus Christ, we need to understand that unless we meet their physical and emotional needs, they aren't going to be open to hearing what we have to say. That is why some of the most successful ministries in the history of Christianity have met physical needs as part of their mission—feeding, clothing, and housing people, as well as working to help solve their personal crises.

Jesus commands each of us to freely give of what we have been given. That means meeting physical, emotional, and other needs as we work to meet their spiritual ones. That means genuinely caring for the people God puts in our lives and meeting their needs freely, just as God freely meets our own needs.

FREELY GIVING TODAY?

Jesus' command, "freely you have received, freely give," didn't end with the disciples. It's just as much in effect for us today as it was for them nearly 2,000 years ago. We live in a different time, a different place, and a different culture, but it's still our Jesus-given responsibility to care for the poor and sick, to take authority over demonic forces, and to give people the Word of God.

When I look around the body of Christ today, I have to wonder about what happened to this idea of freely giving from what we've received. Too many Christians come to church Sunday after Sunday and go to Bible studies week after week, where they just receive and receive and receive some more. But it seems like that's the end of it for most believers. Instead of going out and giving out of the abundance Jesus has given them, they just continue soaking in His goodness and hoarding it for themselves.

It's almost as if they don't understand just what Jesus has given them.

I want to ask you, what do you think you've done to earn your salvation? What have you done to deserve God's blessings? Were you saved because you studied the Bible really hard and once you knew enough, God saved you? Were you saved because you did enough good things in this life to make you acceptable to God?

Were you saved because you went to all the right places, knew all the right people, and did all the right "Christian" things?

If you believe you are saved because of any of those things, then we need to talk, because the honest, straightforward, God-said-it-and-I-believe-it truth is that there isn't one thing you can do to *earn* your salvation, and not one thing you can do to pay for what's already been done for you.

Your being a Christian has *nothing* to do with how good you are, how educated you are, or how worthy you are. It has *everything* to do with the grace and mercy of a God who extended forgiveness and eternal life to you just because of His own goodness.

Freely you have received, freely give. God has freely given us what we couldn't earn, didn't deserve, and couldn't pay off if we were to work for a million years. But He didn't give us this wonderful gift of salvation so that we could just sit around waiting for the sweet by-and-by. He didn't transfer us from the kingdom of darkness into the kingdom of light so we could just kick back and enjoy our personal relationship with Him—or so we could just hang out together talking to one another about how good God is. No, God has given to us—salvation as well as His other gifts—so that we could be a blessing to others.

JUST SPEAK IT!

One of the excuses many Christians use for not freely giving is that they're worried they're going to mess up somehow. They're going to say or do the wrong thing and offend someone. They don't feel confident in their knowledge of the Bible or in good doctrine, so instead of just telling people about what Jesus has given them, they don't say anything at all.

Maybe you've asked questions like these yourself:

"What if I don't say the right thing at the right time?"

"What if I don't know the right Bible text to give someone?"

"What if I'm asked a question about the Bible that I can't answer?"

These excuses remind me a lot of the one Moses threw out when God told him that he had been chosen to lead the people of Israel out of Egyptian captivity. Remember, God had appeared to Moses in the form of a bush that was engulfed in flames, but miraculously wasn't being burned up. Out of the flames came the voice of God, telling Moses that He had seen the misery and oppression His people had been living under and that He was about to do something about it. Then came Moses' mission: "I will send you to Pharaoh that you may bring My people, the children of Israel, out of Egypt" (Exodus 3:10).

Moses had heard God's call, but he was like a lot of us Christians today—he had excuse after excuse after excuse. One went like this: "O my Lord, I am not eloquent, neither before nor since You have spoken to Your servant; but I am slow of speech and slow of tongue" (Exodus 4:10).

But God wasn't going to let Moses off the hook. He had chosen this man to lead the people's exodus out of captivity and slavery, and He wasn't going to let Moses' lack of ability as a speaker change His mind.

You know, I think part of the problem with Christians giving in to their fears—those fears of having the right thing to say—comes from seeing those preachers and pastors and theologians who seem to know every word of the Bible and can tell you what each of them mean. When believers—especially young believers—hear these kinds of people talk about the Bible, they can begin to feel a little inferior, as if they aren't qualified to talk to others about Jesus.

Yes, it's important to study and know the Scriptures and to be prepared, as the apostle Peter put it, to "always be ready to give a defense to everyone who asks you a reason for the hope that is in you" (1 Peter 3:15). But at the same time, we need to stay humble about what we know and what we don't know, realizing that it's not our ability to recite Scripture or debate theology that wins people over.

If there is any winning to be done, it's the Holy Spirit who will take care of that. He just asks us to be faithful to say what we know and leave the results to Him.

How much faith does it take to do that? How much faith does it require to simply tell someone what God has done for you, and leave the results to the Holy Spirit?

Here's an example of what I'm talking about.

One morning at church I was preaching up a storm—I mean really gettin' down with the Word of God! I knew I had that congregation mesmerized because I could hear how quiet they were and how intently they listened. I really believed I had them in the palm of my hand!

After the service, a man approached me and said with a big smile on his face, "I accepted Jesus Christ today!" Now of course I assumed that it was my incredible exegesis of the Scripture that brought this man to a point of seeing he needed Jesus. Then came the humility check.

I asked him, "What led you to Jesus Christ today?" As I stood there just waiting for him to repeat back to me the high points of my wonderful three-point sermon, he said, "Well, when we were taking the offering I dropped the plate. I realized then that if I can't even pass an offering plate, how in the world can I run my own life? So I gave my life to Jesus!"

Imagine that! I had spent hours and hours preparing my sermon, and the Holy Spirit came down and used something as simple as a dropped collection plate to bring this man to the point of knowing he needed Jesus! And what was really humbling about that scene is that we had taken the offering before I'd preached one word.

Jesus never asked His disciples to know every verse and every word of Scripture before they freely gave to others. All He asked them to do was obey Him, to make themselves available to others who had needs, and to open their mouths and speak His name.

Still, you may be asking, "What if I make a mistake?" or "What if I say the wrong thing?" Well, you just might! I don't know if there's anyone who's made it their habit to open their mouths and tell others about Jesus who hasn't at some point said something or done something they wish they could have back. But you can't let your fear of stumbling over your own words and actions keep you from holding high the wonderful name of Jesus.

Not every Christian has read the whole Bible or can quote every Scripture verse that relates to a person's need for Jesus Christ. But there is one thing every believer has, and that is his or her own personal testimony. Each of us can tell the story of what Jesus gave to us when we believed, and the destructive, degrading things He took from us when He set us free by the power of His blood shed for us.

You've heard it before, but I'm going to say it again: There is no book, sermon, or presentation more eloquent or convincing than the message of a changed life. If you can't talk about anything else, you can talk about *that*. And the Holy Spirit will use it in a mighty way, beyond all of your expectations.

Freely giving what you've freely received isn't a matter of having enough knowledge of the Scriptures or doctrine, and it's not a matter of having enough theological training or experience in ministry.

It's a matter of having enough faith to boldly yet humbly tell people about what Jesus has done for us personally and what He can do for them, too.

GIVE...AND GOD WILL MEET YOUR NEEDS

During the course of my ministry, I've heard people say plenty of backward things about their walk with God and their service to Him—things such as, "I'm gonna make enough money so that I can do some missionary work when I retire."

And just *how* backward is that? Think about what Jesus told His disciples as they headed out to minister in His name: "Do not take along any gold or silver or copper in your belts; take no bag for the journey, or extra tunic, or sandals or a staff; for the worker is worth his keep" (Matthew 10:9–10, NIV).

I have to wonder how many Christians today would sign up for that kind of service. How many aspiring missionaries would continue to pursue that career if their churches or the missionary organizations they had signed up with told them, "We aren't giving you anything for your trip—no money, no extra clothing, not even a plane ticket. And not only that, you aren't allowed to take any money of your own. Now God be with you! Good-bye!"

That, for all intents and purposes, is what Jesus said to His disciples as He sent them on their way. He was basically telling these message-bearers that they wouldn't need to take anything with them but the clothes on their backs. He had already charged the people they were going to with taking care of them.

God is really good at compelling people to trust Him, isn't He?

Not all of us are called to be foreign missionaries, and not all of us are called to be pastors. But God still calls us to invest what little faith and little resources we might have and freely give to others. If that means we need money to do the things He's called us to do, He'll find a way to provide it. If it means we need "the right words" to say in order to win someone to Him, then He'll give us those words.

Too many Christians seem to think it's up to them

to make a way to "freely give" in the way God has called them to do it. They seem more interested in studying, working hard, and planning financially than they are in just having enough faith to give of what God has already given them—and what He's promised to give as they walk in obedience to what He's called us to do.

Too many potential ministers and missionaries are more concerned with being financially secure than they are in just doing what God wants them to do. And for those who feel that way, I'd advise them not to be in ministry. Honestly, you couldn't pay me enough money to take the stress and pressure of being pastor at my church. I do it because I know that God has called me to be there, and I love Him too much to do anything less—or anything different—than what He's called me to do and to be.

Being in ministry means making sacrifices—if not financially, then making sacrifices of time and emotions as you give freely to others. That includes both full-time ministry and ministry you take on as a "layperson."

That's why I always tell people that they can't "freely give" to others until they first come to a point of forgetting about the personal benefits of ministry. They can't give like God gives if they're worried and preoc-cupied about how He will make a way to do that.

God has already promised us that He'll meet all our needs as we do the work it takes to bring His message to a hurting and needy world. That's why Jesus told His disciples, "But seek first the kingdom of God and His righteousness, and all these things shall be added to you" (Matthew 6:33).

I've heard it said that an excuse is a lie wrapped in the skin of a reason. It's time for the excuses to stop! If you are gloriously, wonderfully saved, then *you have all the faith you need to tell a world in need of Jesus about it and to freely give to others, just as God has freely given to you.*

FOCUSING ON YOUR OWN RESPONSIBILITY

Jesus had charged His disciples with the responsibility of going out, preaching the gospel, and doing miracles of healing—just as He had been doing, and He summed up that responsibility with the words, "Freely you have received, freely give."

That's a pretty awesome responsibility, isn't it?

But Jesus followed up this charge to the disciples, telling them:

> "Whatever city or town you enter, inquire who in it is worthy, and stay there till you go out. And when you go into a household, greet it. If the household is worthy, let your peace come upon it. But if it is not worthy, let your peace return to you. And whoever will not receive you nor hear your words, when you depart from that house or city, shake off the dust from your feet. Assuredly, I say to you, it will be more tolerable for the land of Sodom and Gomorrah in the day of judgment than for that city!"
>
> MATTHEW 10:11-15

In short, Jesus was telling the disciples that their *only* responsibility was to obediently preach the message and give of what they had received. Beyond that, there was nothing they could do to *make* anyone receive the message.

Jesus wanted the disciples, and us today, to know that there will be people who will reject the message of salvation, who choose to remain lost and on their way to hell.

We live in a world that needs the very same Jesus who has told us, "Freely you have received, freely give."

Everything we have, we owe to Him, and our response to all these gifts should be deep, heartfelt gratitude— the kind of gratitude that motivates us to obediently give to others.

It takes faith to do that, doesn't it?

It takes enough faith to simply get our mouths, our feet, and everything else God has given us moving out and freely giving.

The encouraging truth, my friend, is that you have all the faith you need.

6

ENOUGH FAITH
TO SPEAK THE TRUTH

Every so often I receive phone calls from church leaders from around the country, asking me if I'd be interested in leaving the Seattle area to come and pastor their church.

I'll tell you, some of these boys really put on the hard sell, sometimes starting by telling me that I can name my salary, then moving through a list of fine benefits my family and I would receive from their congregation.

But what most of these men usually *don't* tell me is why they need a new pastor in the first place! They don't tell me that there are a few prominent families in the congregation who have made trouble for every pastor they've had. They don't tell me about the church leadership who wants to control every little thing the pastor does. And they don't tell me about the downside of living and serving in the community where their church is located. Instead, all they want to do is make their presentation in a positive light, without even making mention of the negatives.

How different we are from Jesus! Jesus always spoke the truth, the whole truth, and nothing but the truth—even when He knew how hard it was for people to hear. Do you want a good example? Then read on and see what—by human standards—might be the worst recruiting pitch in all of history.

PREPPING FOR A DIFFICULT MISSION

Jesus had just given the disciples authority over sickness and demons as well as the command, "Freely you have received, freely give." He had told them that there would be folks who welcomed their message as well as those who refused to hear it.

That all sounds easy enough so far, doesn't it? All the disciples had to do was travel around from city to city and village to village preaching, healing the sick, and casting out demons. I don't know about you, but if I heard about an enterprise like that I'd be asking where I could sign up.

Okay, so some people would reject me and the message. I could handle that. I'd do just like Jesus said—shake the dust off my feet and go find someone who wanted to listen. And being sent out with nothing but the clothes on my back? I kind of like that idea. I could get excited about relying on God alone, and watching Him provide for my needs.

But that wasn't the whole job description.

Jesus wasn't finished. Not by a long shot! Now it was time for Him to tell the disciples what they would be facing as they went out to take His message to the Jewish people:

> "Behold, I send you out as sheep in the midst of wolves. Therefore be wise as serpents and harmless as doves. But beware of men, for they will deliver you up to councils and scourge you in their synagogues. You will be brought before governors and kings for My sake, as a testimony to them and to the Gentiles. But when they deliver you up, do not worry about how or what you should speak. For it will be given to you in that hour what you should speak; for it is not you who speak, but the Spirit of your Father who speaks in you."
>
> MATTHEW 10:16–20

Now Jesus had spoken a great many encouraging words to the disciples during His time on earth...but these don't sound like those kinds of words, do they? Right off the bat, He tells them that they would be like sheep among wolves as they went out.

The Bible doesn't tell us whether or not any of the disciples had experience herding sheep, but we know that they lived in a part of the world where sheep ranching was a major part of the economy. They had to know that sheep were very passive animals and that wolves were predators who loved nothing more than to find some defenseless woollies for lunch. They knew that in 100 contests between the sheep and the wolves, the score would be Wolves 100, Sheep 0.

You've probably never heard of a sports team with the name "sheep." Can you imagine the Oakland Raiders up against the Baltimore Sheep? Or the St. Louis Lambs? It just wouldn't work. Sheep have "victim" written all over them.

And that wasn't all. Jesus talked about the very real possibility of the disciples being arrested and brought before the authorities. They could even have been flogged (flogging at that time was a brutal and sometimes fatal form of punishment by whipping), just because they were preaching His name.

YOU'RE TELLING US TO DO WHAT?

I can't help but think that at about that time the disciples must have wondered what they'd gotten themselves into. First Jesus told them to take no provisions—not even spending money—with them on their trip, and now He's telling them that they would be walking among predators, some of whom would love nothing more than to put a stop to their ministries by putting a stop to them.

But Jesus was committed to telling the truth, and He wasn't going to sugarcoat the world's hatred for Him, for His message, *and* for His messengers. He wanted them to understand that people were going to hate them on account of Him, and that they would face persecution and punishment just because they dared to speak the truth.

Jesus sent His disciples out as lambs among wolves, but He didn't want them to be quiet like lambs. No, He wanted them to boldly and wisely preach the gospel, even at great personal risk: "Therefore be as shrewd as snakes and as innocent as doves" (Matthew 10:16, NIV).

This wasn't a case of someone sending out a dozen men under false pretenses. Jesus wanted His disciples to know that people weren't going to necessarily like them and their message.

Can you think of anyone who would know better than Jesus that His message was going to make the disciples unpopular, even hated? Jesus had experienced firsthand what kind of reception His bold preaching on the kingdom of God had generated. The Jewish religious leaders hated Him and wanted Him dead. He was a Savior who bucked a corrupt religious system, who stepped on religious toes, and who openly challenged the way the Jewish people had been living and worshiping for centuries.

Now, He was sending the disciples out to do the same thing.

The world back then hated Jesus' message and His messengers. And it's no different today. We can see in our own nation how the name of Jesus and the teachings of the Bible have become hated, shunned, and banned. The mere mention of His name stirs people to anger. Why are we surprised? We shouldn't expect it to be any other way.

A MESSAGE THE WORLD HATES

There's a watered-down gospel out there today that's giving people a false picture of true Christianity. To listen to this message, you would think that when you accept Jesus Christ, all your troubles will just flow away. There are lots of preachers and teachers on the scene today who tell people how Jesus will save them, forgive them, heal them, and give them a purpose in this life. And it's true! He will! But for some reason, they don't ever seem to get around to telling folks that they will face opposition, ridicule, and even hatred just for living a godly life and for spreading the message of Jesus to the world around them.

The world hates the Christian message today and calls it "narrow-minded" or "too religious." More than anything else, today's culture wants us to compromise our message. It wants us to preach a message like,

"Jesus is *a* way to God," and "If Christianity works for you, then that's great," or "God loves and accepts all people, no matter what kind of lifestyle they live or beliefs they espouse."

When we're walking right, living right, and talking right, we can be sure that people will be coming out of the woodwork to oppose what we're doing and saying. They may mask their hatred as "working for tolerance" or "protecting the constitutional principle of separation of church and state," but the bottom line is that the world opposes our preaching, teaching, and standing for the things of God. It doesn't want to be reminded of its own sinfulness or its need for forgiveness through Jesus Christ.

If you're standing up for the principles of the Word of God and speaking out on behalf of Jesus, then you can be sure that the world will do and say anything it can to get you to shut up. It will threaten you, label you, call you names, accuse you of having all kinds of antisocial views, and paint you as a squinty-eyed, Bible-pounding, fundamentalist wacko. The question we as a church need to address today is this: When the world turns up the heat on us, are we going to fold up our tent, or are we going to continue speaking up?

SOME PEOPLE WHO SPOKE UP

Where would the church of Jesus Christ be today if the apostles had been as weak and soft in their preaching as many modern believers are today? What if Peter, James, Philip, and Paul had concerned themselves more with who liked them than with whom they were serving? Truthfully, I believe that had that happened, the church would have died off in a generation or two.

When you read the book of Acts, you see men who faced some heat from the world, but who weren't worried about the fact that there were lots of people who didn't like them—including people in positions of power. All they did was continue doing what Jesus had told them to do: Preach the word!

You want an example? Take a look at Peter and John. Over and over they were arrested, threatened, harassed, and even beaten because they preached and healed in the name of Jesus. The Jewish leaders did everything they could to shut these boys up about Jesus, but they wouldn't stop. In fact, when they were hauled before the Sanhedrin—the very Jewish council that had sentenced Jesus to death—they openly refused to stop preaching about Jesus: "Judge for yourselves whether it is right in God's sight to obey you rather than God. For we cannot help speaking about what we have seen and heard" (Acts 4:19–20, NIV).

I just love how Peter and John had enough faith and enough courage to tell some very powerful men—men who represented a very real danger to them—that they weren't going to stop preaching no matter what. And I have to wonder if the body of Christ today has that kind of faith and courage. When we are threatened by earthly powers today, do we shrink back and promise not to make waves, or do we continue in obedience to what God tells us to do?

We need that kind of faith and courage in the body of Christ now more than ever. We need men and women who are willing to put their own comfort, safety, and reputations on the line for the kingdom of God. But when we do that, I can guarantee you one thing: We won't be winning any civic awards or praised in the editorial pages of the newspaper. We will be hated.

I know that because Jesus said so. It was true throughout His earthly ministry. That's why He told His men later in this passage, "A disciple is not above his teacher, nor a servant above his master. It is enough for a disciple that he be like his teacher, and a servant like his master. If they have called the master of the house Beelzebub, how much more will they call those of his household!"(Matthew 10:24–25).

In other words, Jesus tells us, the world hates Me, so it's going to hate you, too, because you follow Me and speak the same kind of words I speak.

BEING HATED ON HIS ACCOUNT

I've met a number of Christians who can't seem to understand why the world hates them and their message. They feel stung by the criticism, cynicism, and insults. They seem to have this beaten-down "woe is me" mentality when it comes to dealing with people who are indifferent, or even hostile, to biblical values and the Good News of Christ.

But we can all take encouragement in the fact that Jesus *told us* that's the way it was going to be. Jesus warned the disciples that there would be people in positions of power who would seek to stop them from preaching His message. However, later on in this account, He puts it a little more bluntly: "You will be hated by all for My name's sake" (Matthew 10:22).

Some Christians are disliked just because there's nothing likable about them. They're self-centered or obnoxious or rude. That could be because they haven't been walking with God long enough—or haven't yielded enough control of their lives to Jesus yet. But Jesus isn't talking about people not liking you because you aren't likable—He's talking about people not liking you because your life and your words remind them that they need what you have.

Jesus told the disciples that people were going to hate them, but He wanted them to make sure that they were hated for the right reason: because they were preaching a message that many in power didn't want to hear.

If you were to do a Google search of my name on your computer, you'd see that there are a lot of people saying some very nasty things about me. I've been called a bigot, a homophobe, and I've even been accused of preaching some kind of "Christian jihad"—all because I have the nerve to stand against ungodliness and immorality and stand up for the message of Jesus Christ.

There are times when I feel sorry for my wife and kids. My wife, Pat, has had to put up with a lot of crazy stuff because of the things that go on at Antioch Bible Church, and my kids have had to hear people talk about how their dad is crazy. Even some of the people who attend my church have found themselves a little reluctant to talk about where they attend worship services.

And why is all that?

Because at our church, we have a black-and-white message being preached in a world that is nothing more than different shades of gray.

Jesus told the disciples that "all men" would hate them on account of Him. Now, I've already shown you that the "unsaved" world will hate us because we preach His message. But there's another group of people who might respond the same way.

HATRED FROM OUR OWN RANKS

It may shock you to hear me say it, but when you speak and live according to biblical truth, you might find some hatred and persecution from a source you might not expect: the church itself. That's right! Even the body of Christ, those who are called to live and walk in obedience to God's Word, can and very often do find reason to criticize, ostracize, and dislike the Christian who won't tolerate deviation from the Word of God.

If there's one thing I've noticed about the organized church today, it is that it doesn't like to be disturbed—and likes it even less when its traditions and ways of doing things are challenged. I can tell you that I've lost close friends—some of them fellow preachers—over biblical issues. When I saw that someone was preaching, teaching, or living something I knew was in direct contradiction to the Word of God, then I had to speak up. And while it broke my heart to lose that friendship over it, I knew that Jesus was worth it. I knew that having a body of Christ that holds fast to the principles in the Bible was worth it.

How many believers today have enough faith and enough courage to stand up and speak out when they see things wrong within the body of Christ? How many of us have enough faith to confront sin and immorality within the body? How many of us have enough courage to speak correction when we see that things aren't lining up with the Word?

That is exactly what Jesus did, what He called His disciples to do, and what He wants us to do today!

Some Christians today will tell you, "Well, you can't judge." *Yes, you can!* If you judge based on what the Bible says (not what you think or what others think), you not only can judge but you are *instructed* to judge when you see something wrong in an individual believer's life or within a certain congregation.

A DIVISIVE MESSAGE

Today, even we Christians seem more concerned about "tolerance" than we are about the Word of God. We want to make sure we don't offend anyone by telling them that they're living in sin or that they need to change their behavior if they want to be right with God. Instead, we just want to welcome anyone and everyone into the "family" for a big group hug— even when they have no intention or desire to change.

Jesus was clear as day about the fact that His message wasn't going to unite people: "Brother will deliver up brother to death, and a father his child;

and children will rise up against parents and cause them to be put to death" (Matthew 10:21). Later on, He told them:

> "Do not think that I came to bring peace on earth. I did not come to bring peace but a sword. For I have come to 'set a man against his father, a daughter against her mother, and a daughter-in-law against her mother-in-law.' And 'a man's foes will be those of his own household.'"
>
> MATTHEW 10:34-36

Now this is a little hard to understand, isn't it? Wasn't Jesus called the "Prince of Peace" (Isaiah 9:6)? Didn't He say, "Blessed are the peacemakers" (Matthew 5:9)? What is all this talk of betrayal? What was He really saying when He told the disciples that He had come not to bring peace but a sword?

Jesus came to earth and died so that we sinful humans can have peace with God. But Jesus wanted His followers to understand that this New Covenant teaching and preaching was going to bring conflict— conflict between those who believed His message and acknowledged who He is and those who didn't want to hear His message and would be opposed to it.

But Jesus takes this a step further when He told the disciples in the very next sentence, "He who loves father or mother more than Me is not worthy of Me. And he who loves son or daughter more than Me is not worthy of Me. And he who does not take his cross and follow after Me is not worthy of Me" (Matthew 10:37–38).

Jesus was saying, in other words, that those who were more interested in keeping peace at home than they were in speaking the words and doing the deeds that please Him are not worthy to be counted among His true disciples.

Those are some strong words, brothers and sisters, but they're not my words. They are from the mouth of Jesus Himself.

God has the power to make peace in any situation, but He never wants that peace to come at the cost of compromising His Word or His principles. He doesn't want us as believers to feel like we have to walk on eggshells in order to get along with everyone. Rather, He wants us to speak the truth and to preach a message Jesus Himself said would bring division among people.

Nobody said that living a life that pleases God and speaking the words He wants us to speak—words the world desperately needs to hear—would be easy, least of all Jesus. But God has charged those who follow Him with taking His Word to the world around us, and He's given us both the power and the encouragement we need to do it faithfully.

Do you have enough faith to take a stand for your Lord in the face of opposition or even outright hostility? Yes, you do. The faith that set you free from sin and made you part of God's own family is more than enough to enable you to identify with Jesus in front of a world that hates His name to this very day.

JESUS' WORDS OF ENCOURAGEMENT

While Jesus gave the disciples some very heavy and difficult—not to mention brutally honest—warnings about some of the effects of preaching the gospel, He also gave them some generous helpings of encouragement to overcome their fears and worries over the difficult path they had chosen. A few pages back, we highlighted one of those hopeful promises in Matthew 10:19–20, where Jesus said His followers didn't even have to worry about what to say or how to answer when they are attacked. The Holy Spirit Himself, Jesus told them, would give them the words to say.

The apostle Paul echoed Jesus' encouragement against worry when he wrote, "Be anxious for nothing, but in everything by prayer and supplication, with thanksgiving, let your requests be made known to God" (Philippians 4:6).

A lot of Christians are good at finding things to worry about, and that's why so many of us are so uptight or fearful when it comes to speaking God's truth. But Jesus was telling the disciples very directly that they didn't need to worry when their preaching got them in trouble with the authorities; God Himself, through His Spirit, wasn't only going to help them know what to say, but was going to say it for them.

Jesus knew that the disciples, being human beings with human emotions, might have reason to be afraid of what the worldly powers could do to them because of their testimony for Him. But He reminded them that while the world may be able to do them physical harm, it could never do anything to their souls, simply because they served a God who loved them and cared about them:

> "And do not fear those who kill the body but cannot kill the soul. But rather fear Him who is able to destroy both soul and body in hell. Are not two sparrows sold for a copper coin? And not one of them falls to the ground apart from your Father's will. But the very hairs of your head are all numbered. Do not fear therefore; you are of more value than many sparrows."
>
> MATTHEW 10:28-31

There's something very empowering about not being afraid of being harmed, hated, or even killed by another for what you say, isn't there? That is exactly what Jesus was saying to His twelve disciples—and to us today.

Jesus wants us to boldly and without compromise speak the truth as He has revealed it to us in His written Word. But what does it take to do that? It requires just enough faith to know that every word of His Book is truth. And it also requires enough faith to know that He's got our back when it comes to preaching and teaching the things of God—things that a fallen world won't want to hear and may hate us for saying.

Never doubt it, my friend, you have all the faith you need.

7

A DOUBLE-DOG DARE

don't think there's a man around who has seen the classic holiday movie *A Christmas Story* and didn't smile and nod to himself when the narrator explained the nuances of the playground dare.

First there was the dare, then the double dare. And if that didn't get a kid to do something, there was the double-dog dare, the triple dare, and the dare of all dares, *the triple-dog dare.*

In my neighborhood, a kid was really throwing down the gauntlet when he dropped a double dare on someone. But if you wanted to really get into a guy's head, you gave him the *double*-dog dare—which was almost as serious as talking about his mama, something that always meant trouble. Everybody knew that when it got to the point of a double-dog dare, there was no backing down.

It might sound a little funny to say it in this way, but when it comes to faith, the Bible is filled with all kinds of dares. Over and over we see God just daring those He loves to trust in the One who is big enough to do incredible things with just a little bit of faith. Here's an example: "Test me in this," says the LORD Almighty, "and see if I will not throw open the floodgates of heaven…" (Malachi 3:10, NIV). And over and over and over we see Him doing just that on behalf of people who were strong in the little faith they had, and who set their trust in Him.

What does that kind of faith look like? What kind of faith does it take to respond rightly to God's challenges to trust completely in Him? Well, I *triple*-dog dare you to read on and find out!

DARING TO ASK FOR 'MORE'

When I preach and speak, I sometimes like to refer to biblical characters who demonstrated a deep and powerful faith in their words and actions as "bad boys." These are men who not only believed God, but who also did amazing things because of their faith—things many of us wouldn't have the nerve to do.

The Old Testament books of 1 and 2 Kings contain the stories of a couple of *really* bad boys named Elijah and his main man, Elisha. They were both prophets of God to the nation Israel around the ninth century before Jesus Christ.

Over and over Elijah showed that he was a bad boy, standing tall and strong as a biblical example of faith in action. In 2 Kings 2, he again shows how bad a boy he was when he prepared himself to be taken up to heaven. As he was about to finish his trip from Gilgal to Bethel, where he would leave this planet, he stood with Elisha on the banks of the Jordan River. But instead of wading or taking a boat across the river, Elijah rolled up his cloak and slapped it down on the water. Boom! The Jordan split in two, and he and Elisha crossed on dry land.

Now why do I say Elisha's a bad boy? First of all, when Elijah found out that God was going to take him, he told Elisha to stay behind. But Elisha wasn't having any of that staying-behind stuff. He told Elijah repeatedly, "As the LORD lives, and as your soul lives, I will not leave you!" (2 Kings 2:2, 4, 6).

But Elisha was also a bad boy because as soon as

he and the older prophet had reached the other side of the Jordan, Elijah asked him what he wanted before he was left behind to continue on in the Lord's work. It was sort of a going-away present. And Elisha had the audacity—and the faith—to ask his teacher, "Please let a double portion of your spirit be upon me" (2 Kings 2:9).

Whoa! Some of us might say, "Isn't that a little self-ish, asking for double what Elijah had? That's not being humble! He should have just asked that he could continue Elijah's ministry." Even Elijah seemed a bit taken aback. "You have asked a hard thing," the older prophet said. "Nevertheless, if you see me when I am taken from you, it shall be so for you; but if not, it shall not be so" (2 Kings 2:10).

That's exactly what happened, too. As the two walked together, a chariot and horses of fire suddenly appeared and swept Elijah up to heaven in a whirlwind. At first, Elisha was really upset that his mentor was gone, but it wasn't long before the prophets of Israel recognized that he was the one to take Elijah's place as the nation's leading prophet and miracle worker.

Elisha was a bad boy because he dared to believe

God and dared to ask for more of His Spirit. But as his ministry got rolling, he met a woman who was every bit as bad as he was.

ONE "BAD GIRL" OF THE FAITH

The book of 2 Kings tells us that Elisha often traveled to a town called Shunem, where he met an unnamed but wealthy woman who went out of her way to show him some hospitality.

At first, she just invited him to have a bite to eat with her and her husband, but later, she wanted to take the hospitality up a notch: "And she said to her husband, 'Look now, I know that this is a holy man of God, who passes by us regularly. Please, let us make a small upper room on the wall; and let us put a bed for him there, and a table and a chair and a lampstand; so it will be, whenever he comes to us, he can turn in there" (2 Kings 4:9–10).

On one of his trips to Shunem, Elisha went to his room, and as he lay resting it occurred to him that he should repay this Shunammite for her hospitality. He told his servant Gehazi to bring the woman to his room, where he asked her through Gehazi, "Look, you have been concerned for us with all this care. What can I do for you? Do you want me to speak on your behalf to the king or to the commander of the army?'" (2 Kings 4:13).

I don't know about you, but if a powerful man of God like Elisha asked what he could do for me, I might have whipped out a long list of things. I like driving high-performance cars, so I might have suggested a new Lamborghini. And I travel quite a bit to do speaking engagements, so it might be nice to have a private jet. And while we're at it, I wouldn't mind having a chance to meet and talk with the president.

But this woman gave Elisha—the man who had the power and authority to give her just about anything she wanted—an incredible response: "I dwell among my own people," she said (2 Kings 4:13). In other words, she was content with her home and her family. She had everything she needed.

There was, however, one thing she didn't mention. It was something that all Jewish women wanted very much in that culture: a child. And because she demonstrated that she was content when it came to what she needed, she was about to get what she wanted.

FAITH...AND CONTENTMENT

Living a life of real faith means, among many other things, learning to be content with what you have, knowing that God will meet your every need. It is only when you live and walk in that kind of contentment that God will be freed to give to you beyond your needs, providing you with some of those deeply felt heart desires—the very things you hadn't dared to ask for.

After that unnamed Shunammite woman had left Elisha, he had another little talk with Gehazi and asked him what they could do to repay their hostess for her generous hospitality. Elisha knew she was content with life. But he wanted to reward her for her kindness to a man of God.

Now apparently Gehazi had spent some time around this woman and her husband and had found out that they had no children. He told Elisha, "Actually, she has no son, and her husband is old" (2 Kings 4:14).

If you know anything about Jewish culture during biblical times (and that includes the New Testament era), you know that it was a shameful thing for a woman not to have children. Elizabeth, for example, the future mother of John the Baptizer, was a barren woman past childbearing years. But when she learned that a miracle baby was on the way, she cried out, "The Lord has done this for me. In these days he has shown his favor and taken away my disgrace from among the people" (Luke 1:25, NIV).

Elisha told Gehazi to bring the woman back, and when she stood in the doorway of Elisha's room, he spoke to her. This time, directly. What he gave her was a promise from God that must have blown her mind: "About this time next year you shall embrace a son" (2 Kings 4:16).

This woman's reaction to Elisha's promise is priceless: "No, my lord. Man of God, do not lie to your maidservant!" (v. 16). When I read this, I can just hear her saying, "Don't play with my head! I just told you that I'm content in my life now. If you really mean this then—oh!—by all means do it, but if you're just messing with me, I might have to ask you to leave my house."

But Elisha wasn't teasing her. He was delivering a solemn promise of God. And true to God's word, the once-barren woman became pregnant and about a year later gave birth to a son.

God dares each of us to be like the Shunammite woman who was blessed in a way she never expected, simply because she was content with what God had already given her. When we choose contentment, we've opened the door for God to bless us even beyond our immediate needs.

WHEN A DESIRE GIVES BIRTH TO A NEED

There is apparently a pretty big gap of time covered between verses 17 and 18 in 2 Kings 4. When we leave verse 17, the Shunammite woman had just given birth to the son Elisha had promised her. As we leave verse 18, that son had grown up enough to be able to go out to his father, who was in one of his fields with his hired hands.

The news the boy had for his father that day wasn't good. He complained of a terrible headache, one so bad that his father ordered one of his servants to take the lad to his mother. As it turns out, this was no ordinary Tylenol headache—the boy died while he was sitting in his mother's lap.

You have to wonder what kind of grief a mother would feel to have her only child—her miracle baby—die so suddenly in her arms like that. But as we read this text, this mother seems to be a picture of calm and peace, as well as faith, in the midst of an awful situation. She simply took the boy up to Elisha's room, then called on her husband and asked him to send one of the servants and a donkey so she could go to Elisha and bring him back to her son's side.

Her husband couldn't figure out why she was taking off for Mount Carmel at that particular moment. What was the urgency? What was the occasion?

"Why are you going to him today?" he asked.

"It is well," she said (v. 23).

When Elisha saw her in the distance, he was puzzled. He sent his servant ahead to see if everything was all right.

"It is well," she said (v. 26).

But when she reached the prophet, Scripture says she got down on her knees and took hold of his feet. "Did I ask a son of my lord? Did I not say, 'Do not deceive me'?" she said (v. 28).

Realizing that her miracle boy had died, Elisha's plan was to send his servant with his staff to lay on the boy's face and bring him back to life. But the Shunammite woman wasn't going to let Elisha out of her sight. She said, "As the LORD lives and as your soul lives, I will not leave you" (v. 30). So Elisha got to his feet and followed her home, went up into the prophet's chamber where the little boy lay dead, and called him back into life by the power of God.

On the day her little son died, did this woman need "more faith" to see an awesome miracle of life in her family? No, she simply took the tiny faith seed that she possessed and planted it in the power and faithfulness of the God of Elisha.

"*Please send me one of the young men and one of the donkeys,*" she calmly said to her husband, even though the worst thing she could imagine had just hit her household.

"*It is well,*" she told him, even as events seemed to be spinning wildly out of control.

"*It is well,*" she told Elisha's servant, even though she was in the middle of the greatest crisis of her life. No weeping, wailing, and carrying on. She simply took her stand on the little faith that she possessed, and waited for Elisha's God to do the impossible.

Now most everyone who loses a loved one to death

would love to see that person resurrected and whole again. What gave this woman the faith to believe *her* boy would be alive again before that day was through? It was just this: She had never asked for a son. She had been content with the life God had given her. But then God chose to promise her a baby, and graced her with the very thing she so deeply desired but never requested. A baby. A man-child. And this mother did not believe God would fail to keep His promise of a son to raise and to love for the rest of her life.

What is God's dare to each one of us? To have more faith? No. I think His dare is to be strong in the faith that we have—no matter how small it may seem to us. He dares us to remain as calm as this woman was when we find ourselves in the middle of a personal crisis, knowing that He is in perfect control no matter how bad the situation looks. I believe He double dares each of us to plant that tiny seed of faith, not allowing ourselves to be shaken by circumstances. And He double-dog dares us to simply rest in His promises and in His love for us, even when it seems He's a thousand miles away.

Earlier, I pointed out how easy it is for most Christians to talk a good game of trusting God and believing His promises when things are going well. But the second some kind of difficulty arises in our lives, many of us just lose it. When we lose a job, a relationship, or our health, we allow anxiety to run wild in our lives, and expose our hearts to the flaming arrows of the evil one.

But it's during difficult times that God does His best work in our lives. When we're really up against it, we realize that Jesus is not just all we need, but maybe all we've got. I like to say that when we hit bottom, Jesus is right there with us, and that gives us a great place to push off from.

That is exactly how this unnamed Shunammite woman handled her situation: by going to the one she knew was as well-connected with God as anyone she would ever know.

DON'T SETTLE FOR "PLAN B"

Elisha had a plan for bringing back this woman's son, but it wasn't her plan at all. Initially, the prophet told Gehazi to tuck in his cloak, take Elisha's staff, and go ahead to Shunem to deal with the situation. But that just wasn't going to do for this woman of faith: *"As the LORD lives and your soul lives, I will not leave you!"*

She hadn't come for Plan B but for Plan A, which was for this man of God to come and meet her need. In other words, she wasn't going to settle for Gehazi when Elisha was available. She hadn't come for Gehazi, and she hadn't come for Elisha's staff. There was nothing wrong with either, but she had come for Elisha himself, and she wasn't going to go anywhere until he agreed to come with her.

And that is what he did. But it was only after Gehazi failed to raise the boy that Elisha went into action himself. Gehazi had done just as Elisha had told him and laid the staff across the boy's face. But when he came out of the house, the boy was still stone dead. Only after Elisha reached the house did the woman from Shunem receive what she wanted and needed.

Now let me ask you a question. What would have happened if that woman had settled for Gehazi instead of Elisha, the man of God? Her son would have remained dead! She knew, even before Elisha did, that Gehazi wasn't going to cut it. That's why she didn't stay with Gehazi, but instead left her home and went back to Elisha.

As I've read this passage, I've asked myself how many Christians settle for Gehazis when they could have Elishas? How many of us settle for church-as-usual, for denominationalism, for religion, when we could have more of Jesus Christ? How many of us settle for our own Plan Bs when God has a wonderful, amazing Plan A—if we dare to take what little faith we have and step out on it?

You see, when we go to God, we don't go just to receive forgiveness. We don't go just to receive His blessings. No, we seek out God Himself, and when we do that, we receive the good things—the perks, the privileges, and the blessings—that come along with knowing Him.

Our part in the bargain is only this: having just enough faith to believe Him.

ENOUGH FAITH TO "TOUCH 'EM ALL"

The greatest faith in the world is the faith it takes to come to Jesus Christ for forgiveness and salvation. And while it might sound a little strange for me to say it, from that moment it's all downhill. In other words, if you've got enough faith to believe that God will forgive you and accept you into His kingdom, you've got all the faith you need to live the life He wants you to live and to do the things He wants you to do.

Living a life of real faith in Jesus Christ is a lot like running the bases in a baseball game after someone else has hit a home run. Most of us know that after a batter hits a home run, all he has to do to put the runs on the scoreboard is trot around the bases, making sure he touches every bag along the way. If he doesn't touch every base, he can still be thrown out by the defense. As one announcer used to cry out when his team hit a home run, "Touch 'em all!"

We've got the greatest power hitter in all of history on our side, and His name is Jesus Christ. Every swing He takes on our behalf is a home run, and all that leaves for us to do is run the bases. He's done the hard part, and our only responsibility is to make sure we run the bases and touch every base.

Too many Christians are like a baseball player who hits a home run then slides into every base, including home plate, on the way around the diamond. By the time he comes home, he's exhausted! He could have just taken a leisurely stroll around the bases. Not only that, his teammates would wonder if he'd lost his mind!

A life of faith can be an incredible experience, but it isn't complicated. It's simply a matter of seeking after God and His righteousness with everything you are. And it's also a matter of not being willing to settle for anything less than Him.

That's the dare God has for all of us today.

When you take God up on that dare, you become the beneficiary of all His promises, every one of which He keeps faithfully. But not only that, you get to make a difference in the lives of those around you.

A DARING—AND INFECTIOUS—FAITH

Mark chapter 2 tells the story of some guys who dared to step out in faith, and the part they played in the amazing healing of a friend. The scene was a crowded house in the town of Capernaum, where Jesus was teaching a not-even-standing-room crowd.

Jesus always drew crowds. Some followed Him because they wanted something from Him. A meal. A miracle. A handout. While there's nothing wrong with wanting those things, following Jesus just for those blessings truly is settling for second best. There were a few who followed Him just because they wanted to be near Him, to hear His teaching, and to be a part of what He was doing. And there were even a few who followed because they had enough faith to believe that He could do something for those they cared about.

One evening, outside a home in Capernaum, there was a group of men who followed Jesus because they wanted something—not for themselves, but for a friend in need. Their friend was a paralytic, so helpless that his buddies had to pack him around on a mat.

These boys were faced with a problem: They couldn't get in the house because it was already full. But what looked like a barrier to getting their friend to Jesus was for them only a small inconvenience. They believed Jesus could do something for their friend, and they weren't going to let something as minor as a crowded house keep them from getting him in Jesus' presence.

They, like the woman from Shunem, weren't going to take no for an answer. They weren't going to settle for anything less than the very best God could give them and their friend that night.

In chapter 2, I pointed out that sometimes we need to forget about etiquette and decorum when it comes to demonstrating enough faith to get something done. That's exactly what these four fellas did. Instead of politely asking the crowd in the house to part so they could get in, and instead of sending a message to Jesus, they got up on top of the house and tore a hole in it so they could drop their boy down to the floor where Jesus was sitting.

WITH FRIENDS LIKE THESE...

These are the kind of friends you want when your chips are down. These are the kind of brothers you want in your corner! If I ever got so sick I couldn't even reach out to Jesus for myself, I would want friends ready to tear a hole in the wall of heaven to get me in front of Jesus. And what's more, I not only hope I can have such a friend, I hope I can *be* such a friend.

But there's a question this story poses for all of us today. Why is it that so many of us, when we're given the opportunity to demonstrate our faith on behalf of those in need, give up and bail out so easily? You may not like my answer—but I've never been accused of being a shrinking violet. I think it's because we're too selfish and too weak in our faith.

These four men had enough faith and determination to rearrange the roof in that house to get their friend to the One they knew could heal him. Most homes in that culture shared a wall with the next home in the line. That meant these guys probably had to lift their friend up on the roof, then carry him a good distance—overcoming several barriers—before they were over the house where Jesus was teaching.

Don't miss the Lord's response to all this! Mark reports, "When Jesus saw their faith, He said to the paralytic, 'Son, your sins are forgiven you'" (2:5). A few moments later, He got down to what this afflicted man's friends wanted in the first place. He said, "Arise, take up your bed, and go your way to your house" (v. 11).

Some Christians today make the mistake of thinking that the difficulties they're going through are because God is unhappy with them—or that they don't have enough faith to allow Him to heal them. But the truth of the matter is that sometimes God allows these things to happen to us so that His power and authority over sickness and death can be put on display for everyone to see. What's our part? Putting just a little bit of faith in our big God.

Sometimes we have the opportunity to demonstrate that faith on behalf of another. The faith Jesus responded to that night in Capernaum wasn't that of the disabled man laying on the mat, but the faith his friends dared to have. They used this faith to do something bold and outrageous to get their friend in front of the One they knew could heal him.

What bold and outrageous things are you willing to do to get people in front of Jesus? How much faith does it take to simply take someone by the hand to bring them to the only One who can save, heal, and restore?

You see, God wants to be a blessing to each and every one of His people, and He wants us to make sure that He can bless those He brings into our lives—our friends, our coworkers, our families, even those we might consider "just acquaintances."

But He wants to do that not just because we have what we might think of as "big faith." No, He wants to do that because we have a little faith in a big God who alone has the power and authority to forgive us, cleanse us, welcome us into His kingdom, and bless us and others—just because we believe Him.

The question you have to ask yourself is this: Am I willing to settle for anything less than Jesus Christ Himself? Am I going to look to anything or anyone but Him as I seek to find my way through this sometimes confusing maze called life? Here's a little secret that's worth the whole price of this book: If you are willing to put every little bit of the faith you have in Him, and if you're willing to put everything else aside and follow after Him and Him alone, then you will receive His very best.

C'mon! I dare you to put your tiny little faith into action and simply believe Him and seek Him with everything you have. I double-dog dare you!

The great news, my friend, is that you have all the faith you need.

Also available from
Ken Hutcherson

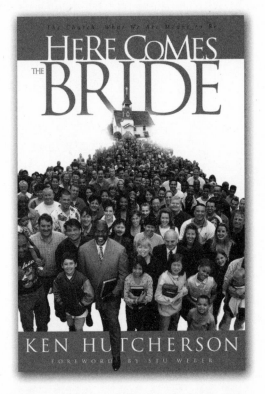

Pastor Ken Hutcherson calls us to the book of Acts to find a church that's bold, energetic, empowered, and unstoppable...and shows how believers can transform today's church according to God's holy plan.

Multnomah® Publishers *Keeping Your Trust...One Book at a Time*®